UFO Crash Sites

Aliens, UFOs, and Cryptids: Unraveling the Unknown, Volume 66

Jade Summers

Published by Jade Summers, 2024.

While every precaution has been taken in the preparation of this book, the publisher assumes no responsibility for errors or omissions, or for damages resulting from the use of the information contained herein.

UFO CRASH SITES

First edition. October 20, 2024.

Copyright © 2024 Jade Summers.

Written by Jade Summers.

Unveiling the Secrets: A Journey Through UFO Crash Sites

Introduction

Delve into the hidden history of UFO crash sites around the globe. This investigation unearths the mysteries and controversies surrounding these enigmatic events, chronicling eyewitness testimonies, government cover-ups, and the relentless pursuit of the truth by researchers and enthusiasts alike.

Chapter 1: The Roswell Incident

1.1 Origins of the Myth

As the phenomenon of Unidentified Flying Objects (UFOs) continues to fascinate and perplex audiences around the globe, the origins of the myths surrounding UFO crash sites offer a captivating insight into human psychology, cultural narratives, and the intersection of science and the unknown. This investigation into the roots of the myth of UFO crash sites reveals not only the evolution of societal fears and hopes but also the ways in which these alleged incidents reflect broader historical contexts.

The tale of UFO crash sites can trace its origins back to the mid-20th century, a time defined by rapid technological advancement and intense geopolitical tension, particularly in the wake of World War II. The dawn of the atomic age brought not only new inventions but also a sense of vulnerability and fear regarding the future of humanity. It was within this framework that eyewitness accounts and conspiracy theories began to take hold, fundamentally altering our cultural landscape.

Influential Incidents

Several key incidents helped solidify the myth of UFO crash sites:

- **Roswell Incident (1947)**: Perhaps the most famous of all UFO crash stories, this event involved the recovery of debris from what was initially reported as a "flying disc" by the military. Although the government eventually claimed it was a weather balloon, the seeds of conspiracy were firmly planted.

- **Kecksburg Incident (1965)**: Witnesses reported seeing a fireball streaking across the sky, followed by the recovery of an acorn-shaped object by military personnel. This incident prompted speculation about a government cover-up.

- **Shag Harbor (1967)**: In Nova Scotia, Canada, a supposed UFO crashed into the harbor, leading to an extensive investigation by the Royal Canadian Mounted Police, further intensifying public interest in these mysterious events.

These incidents became the scaffolding upon which countless conspiracies and narratives were built, each adding layers of complexity to the UFO mythos.

Cold War Context

The tension of the Cold War era played a significant role in nurturing the UFO crash mythology. Citizens were increasingly paranoid about espionage and technological advancements. The idea that extraterrestrial forces could be involved fed into existing fears of the unknown. It catalyzed narratives where not only were aliens a possibility, but so too were government secrets latent in their alleged crashes.

The Media's Role

The media has been pivotal in propagating the myth. Magazines, television shows, and later the internet served to disseminate stories, often blurring the lines between fact and fiction. The soft science of UFOology became a staple of both sensational journalism and academic inquiry. Key factors include:

- **Documentaries & Books**: Publications like "Chariots of the Gods?" by Erich von Däniken challenged the status quo, suggesting an extraterrestrial influence on human civilization, thereby creating a fertile ground for UFO narratives.

- **Television Shows**: Programs such as "The X-Files" and countless others featured narratives that glamorized UFOs, influencing public perception and offering a thrilling escape into the world of conspiracy theories.

Folklore and Urban Legends

Like other legendary narratives, tales of UFO crash sites often assimilated cultural folklore elements. Investors, researchers, and enthusiasts reveled in the intricate web of stories designed to entertain and intrigue. Smaller, localized legends emerged, conveying local lore that blended communities with broader themes of alien encounters.

The Psychology of Belief

At a psychological level, the belief in UFO crash sites taps into a deep-seated yearning for understanding the unknown. For believers and skeptics alike, these theories fuel:

- **Curiosity**: What lies beyond our world?
- **Mystery**: The allure of the unexplained entices people to delve deeper into the unknown.
- **Fear**: Understanding, or at least speculating about, what menace might lurk beyond Earth can be a coping mechanism for existential worries.

Conclusion

The origins of the myth surrounding UFO crash sites are a tapestry woven from historical events, sociopolitical turmoil, and human imagination. Each thread represents a reaction to the unknown and a desire to find meaning in what remains unexplained. As myths persist and evolve, they reflect not only our fear of extraterrestrial life but also expose deeper existential truths about humanity's relationship with the cosmos. With each passing year, these narratives grow richer and more intertwined, captivating the minds of UFO enthusiasts, conspiracy theorists, and researchers alike.

1.2 The Military Response

The aftermath of alleged UFO crashes has always been steeped in a shroud of secrecy and confusion, particularly concerning the military's response to such events. Throughout history, numerous crashes and mysterious sightings have led to heightened scrutiny and speculation regarding how military entities handle the residual debris and any potential extraterrestrial occupants. The veil of opacity surrounding these cases often generates more questions than answers.

When a report of a UFO crash emerges, the military's immediate action is typically methodical and calculated. Key components of their response often include:

- **Assessment of the situation:** Military personnel are dispatched to evaluate the site of the crash. This initial assessment aims to determine whether it poses any threat to national security or public safety.
- **Securing the perimeter:** Following the assessment, the area is cordoned off to prevent unauthorized access. This is vital not only for evidence preservation but also to control potential public panic or curiosity.
- **Gathering intelligence:** Armed with reconnaissance data from military aircraft or satellites, teams work to collect as much information about the incident as possible. This can involve both human intelligence (HUMINT) from eyewitness accounts and technical intelligence (TECHINT)

from radar and surveillance systems.

The most famous case that showcases the military's response to a UFO incident is the Roswell crash of 1947. Initially reported as a "flying disc" by the Roswell Army Air Field, the story quickly evolved into one of cover-ups and conspiracy theories. The military hastened to retrieve the wreckage, and what began with excitement contorted into a narrative of denial.

The Roswell Incident

The military's management of the Roswell incident reflects a broader pattern in how UFO crashes are dealt with:

1. Immediate Public Relations Crisis Management:

Roman officials quickly issued a press release claiming to have recovered a "flying disc," creating a media frenzy.

Hours later, the narrative shifted dramatically, with the military claiming the debris was merely from a downed weather balloon. This pivot was the beginning of many theories suggesting a deliberate obfuscation.

2. Handling of Witnesses:

Witnesses reported being approached by military personnel, with some stating they were threatened with repercussions should they discuss what they had seen.

Such tactics have led to allegations of systematic silencing by officials, giving rise to a pervasive culture of doubt and conspiracy.

Beyond Roswell, additional incidents provide insight into the military's ongoing responses to UFO crashes:

- **The Kecksburg Incident (1965):** Witnesses in Pennsylvania reported a fireball and subsequent landing in the woods. The U.S. Army cordoned off the area and was said to have taken the wreckage, with many later alleging a cover-up of alien technology.

- **The Rendlesham Forest Incident (1980):** American military personnel stationed in the UK observed unexplained lights and encountered an unusual metallic object. The air force conducted an investigation, and while official statements categorized the phenomenon as misinterpretation, testimonies from those involved suggest more than meets the eye.

Patterns of Secrecy

Patterns emerge not only in specific incidents but also in the military's overarching approach to UFO-related cases:

- **Denial and Distraction:** Plans often include immediate denial of extraterrestrial activity and suggest mundane explanations, leveraging official narratives to dominate public discourse.

- **Monumental Indifference to Public Interest:** Despite widespread fascination with UFOs, the military often takes a stance of indifference, leading the public to seek out information through unofficial channels, amplifying conspiracy theories.

- **Creation of Specialized Agencies:** Over time, the military has established various departments like Project Blue Book and more recently AATIP (Advanced Aerospace Threat Identification Program) to study unidentified aerial phenomena (UAPs), albeit its findings remain largely classified.

The Lingering Questions

As we delve deeper into the history of UFO crash sites, the military response continues to trigger an essential question: why the secrecy? And what do they truly know about these unexplained phenomena? The convergence of military involvement and UFO sightings often suggests implications that go beyond mere speculation.

The military's response to UFO crash sites remains a convoluted tapestry of action and reaction, reputation management, and, most significantly, a reflection of broader societal concerns about safety, security, and what lies beyond our understanding of the universe. As enthusiasts, historians, and conspiracy theorists sift through the layered accounts of these incidents, our quest for understanding may uncover truths previously shrouded in secrecy.

1.3 Media Frenzy and Aftermath

The fallout from reports of alleged UFO crashes often engenders a sensationalized media frenzy that magnifies public interest while muddying the waters of factual inquiry. The aftermath of these incidents is as varied as the accounts of the crashes themselves, often leaving an indelible mark on societal perceptions of extraterrestrial life and government transparency.

When a UFO incident breaks into the public consciousness, news outlets, both mainstream and fringe, spring into action. Headlines screaming about "secret government cover-ups" and "extraterrestrial technology" dominate the discourse, leading to a whirlwind of speculation. The 1947 Roswell incident is a prime example of how a story can evolve from a military weather balloon recovery into an enduring legend of UFO research.

Media Coverage Dynamics

The media's response typically follows a predictable arc:

- **Initial Reports**: The first wave of coverage often involves local newspapers or radio stations, which may receive tips

from witnesses or military personnel.
- **Exploitation by National Outlets**: As public interest peaks, larger media organizations pick up the story, often sensationalizing the details to drive viewership and readership.
- **Expert Opinions**: Coverage includes interviews with conspiracy theorists, scientists, and former military officials, adding to the cacophony of differing viewpoints.
- **Debunking Efforts**: Not long after, skeptics and government representatives emerge, attempting to deliver counter-narratives that downplay or discredit the initial reports.

The stark contrast between pro-UFO and skeptical discourse highlights the polarized views on these incidents, often viewed through the lens of belief systems rather than factual analysis. This intricate dance between media portrayal and public perception shapes the legacy of each crash site.

Memorable Cases and Their Media Impact

Consider the following notable UFO crash sites and their aftermaths:

- **Roswell, New Mexico (1947)**: Initially, the press reported the recovery of a "flying disc," only to have the U.S. military quickly claim it was a weather balloon. The discord between initial excitement and official debunking has fueled radio shows, documentaries, and books that delve into what many believe to be a cover-up, solidifying Roswell's status as a hallmark of UFO lore.
- **Kecksburg, Pennsylvania (1965)**: Witnesses described a "fireball" streaking through the sky, followed by reports of a

crash and military presence. National coverage led to increased public pressure for transparency, resulting in decades-long investigations by UFO enthusiasts and significant media documentation.

- **Shag Harbour, Nova Scotia (1967)**: The media frenzy surrounding the mysterious crash in Shag Harbour sparked a flood of local interest and drew attention from national outlets, ultimately leading to an official investigation that remains in the public record, yet continues to confound researchers.

Public Fascination and its Consequences

The aftermath of these incidents often extends beyond mere fascination. Each event becomes a portal into the realm of speculative inquiry, haunting both casual observers and dedicated investigators alike. Additionally, they can impact societal and cultural perceptions in various ways:

- **Increased Government Secrecy**: Following high-profile incidents, governments may increase their surveillance and information-control mechanisms, leading to widespread suspicion.
- **Activism and Advocacy**: Groups demanding government transparency, like The Disclosure Project, emerged from the desire to unveil alleged government cover-ups. Activism grows in intensity, fueled by the belief that more information is being withheld than is shared.
- **Subsequent Documentaries and Literature**: The ensuing media frenzy often creates a market for books, documentaries, and even online forums, further perpetuating the mystery surrounding each crash site.

Conclusion

As these narratives unfold in real-time, they take on a life of their own, transcending the boundaries of their origin. Each incident affects everything from local culture to global discussions about the existence of extraterrestrial life. Consequently, the media frenzy becomes a fundamental aspect of the lore surrounding UFO crash sites, propelling them into the tapestry of modern mythology. The aftermath is not just about what was or wasn't declassified by the government; it's a reflection of humanity's enduring quest for answers in a universe that can often feel unfathomable. This ongoing saga continues to challenge both researchers and enthusiasts, prompting them to sift through layers of sensationalism to uncover the potential truths lurking beneath the headlines.

Chapter 2: Kecksburg and the Acorn

2.1 Eyewitness Accounts

Eyewitness accounts play a pivotal role in the investigation of UFO crash sites, providing compelling narratives that often serve as the foundation for larger investigations into the phenomena. These firsthand experiences can offer unique insights and raise more questions than answers, especially concerning the eyewitnesses' credibility, the circumstances surrounding the sightings, and the implications of their reports.

Unveiling the Testimonies

Over the decades, numerous individuals have come forward, narrating their experiences of witnessing what they claim were UFO crashes. These accounts span decades and have emerged from various regions globally, adding layers of complexity to the investigation of UFO phenomena. Eyewitness testimony can be categorized into several notable aspects:

- **Diversity of Witnesses**: Eyewitnesses range from military personnel and law enforcement officers to civilians and children. The varied backgrounds often lend credibility to their accounts.
- **Contextual Factors**: Accounts often arise in specific contexts—during military exercises, in remote areas with

limited human activity, or amidst local lore that suggests the presence of unexplained aerial phenomena.
- **Corroboration**: Numerous accounts may share similar details or be corroborated by multiple witnesses, enhancing the overall credibility of the narratives.

Notable Cases of Eyewitness Accounts

Many cases stand out in UFO crash history due to detailed eyewitness accounts that lend weight to the investigation. A few prominent examples include:

- **Roswell, New Mexico (1947)**: Perhaps the most famous case in UFO history. Initial reports by army personnel suggested the recovery of a "flying disc," only to be followed by a retraction stating it was a weather balloon. Eyewitnesses like Jesse Marcel, an intelligence officer, described unusual debris that did not resemble anything known at the time.

- **Kecksburg, Pennsylvania (1965)**: Residents reported seeing a fireball crash in the woods. Mary D'Andrea'detailed her encounter of a metallic object resembling an acorn with strange hieroglyphics on its surface. Military personnel reportedly arrived shortly after to secure the area, but many residents were left in confusion about what they had witnessed.

- **The Cash-Landrum Incident (1980)**: Betty Cash and Vickie Landrum claimed to have encountered a diamond-shaped object emitting flames. Their subsequent health issues led them to seek compensation, further complicating their testimonies with elements of personal consequences that must be considered during analysis.

Analyzing Credibility

While many eyewitness accounts have profoundly affected UFO crash investigations, the question of credibility cannot be overlooked. Analysis of these accounts typically involves assessing:

- **Consistency**: Consistent reports among multiple witnesses increase reliability. For instance, when different eyewitnesses at the same location report similar details independently, the likelihood of truth increases.
- **Timing**: Accounts that arise close to the event often have greater validity than those that emerge years later. Over time, memories may become distorted, leading to inaccuracies.
- **Psychological Factors**: Individuals may be influenced by media portrayals or social pressures, impacting their recounting of events—especially those of a highly sensational nature.

The Role of Skepticism

Skepticism plays an essential role in the investigation of UFO crash sites. While many eyewitnesses aim to share their experiences, skeptics often evaluate such accounts through a more critical lens, asking:

- What external factors may have influenced the report?
- Are there alternative explanations for the phenomena observed?
- How does the anecdotal evidence align with known historical data?

Understanding these dynamics allows researchers to sift through claims, separating anecdotal experiences from those that can be corroborated by physical evidence or further research.

Conclusion

Eyewitness accounts provide foundational narratives in the study of UFO crash sites, enriching our understanding of these mysterious events. They bring forth diverse perspectives, each contributing to the collective inquiry into incidents that have intrigued humanity for decades. Nonetheless, as engaging as these stories are, they must be approached with an analytical mindset that weighs both their inherent value and potential biases.

In the end, eyewitness testimonies serve not just to complicate the inquiry of UFO crashes, but also to illuminate the profound desire of individuals to connect with the unknown. They open doors to exploration, investigation, and ultimately, a greater understanding of our place in the cosmos.

2.2 The Unsolved Mystery

The journey into the realm of UFO crash sites often leads to crossroads of fact and fiction, where tantalizing revelations intersect with profound ambiguities. Amid various confirmed incidents, certain occurrences are enveloped in mystery, evoking intrigue, skepticism, and a touch of the fantastic.

One such enigmatic site is the Roswell incident of 1947, an event that has become synonymous with UFO lore. While the U.S. military initially claimed to have recovered a "flying disc," the narrative quickly morphed into that of a weather balloon. This swift pivot left many questioning the authenticity of the explanation, with theorists suggesting deeper governmental conspiracies at play. Thought to have been a simple misidentification, the Roswell affair birthed a multitude of speculations and theories:

- **Alien bodies:** Claims of extraterrestrial entities being recovered alongside the debris have intensified the mystique surrounding Roswell.
- **Secret military experiments:** Some researchers posited that the crashed object might have been involved in top-secret projects, further fostering speculation about government cover-ups.

However, Roswell is merely one case in a broader pattern of incidents that push the boundaries of what we consider ordinary. Among the intricate tapestry of UFO crash sites, there are at least four notable cases that remain unresolved, leaving modern investigators in a quagmire of questions.

Kecksburg, Pennsylvania (1965)

The Kecksburg incident is another compelling narrative in the annals of UFO crashes. On December 9, 1965, thousands witnessed a fiery object streaking across the sky before it supposedly crashed in the woods near Kecksburg. Eyewitness accounts describe a bell-shaped object adorned with strange markings. Shortly after, military units appeared, cordoning off the area and removing the object, leading to theories poised between intrigue and skepticism:

- **High-level cover-up:** Why such a heavy military presence for what was ostensibly a meteor or space debris?
- **Similarities to Nazi technology:** Some UFO enthusiasts speculate the object may have shared characteristics with advanced weaponry developed during World War II.

Aztec, New Mexico (1948)

Another unresolved event in UFO history occurred near Aztec, New Mexico, shortly after the Roswell incident. According to claims by local residents, a craft crash-landed, leading investigators to believe it was a concentrated effort of governmental secrecy. The supposed recovery included descriptions of alien bodies and advanced technology. Key elements of the Aztec incident include:

- **Diverse witness testimonies:** From farmers to police officers, numerous individuals reported seeing the crash site.
- **Conflicting narratives:** Despite the tantalizing nature of the tales, consistency remains elusive, creating a fog of uncertainty around the event.

Pine Ridge Reservation, South Dakota (1977)

In 1977, the Pine Ridge Reservation was reportedly the site of a UFO crash. Witnesses described a luminous object descending before disappearing behind the hills. Eyewitness accounts suggested that the military again exhibited rapid interest in the incident, fueling claims of hidden motives at play. Aspects that contribute to its enigmatic aura include:

- **Native American folklore:** The Oglala Lakota believe the site has spiritual significance, complicating interpretations rooted in modern UFO narratives.
- **Military presence:** Just like earlier cases, the rapid arrival of armed forces sparked speculation about what truly transpired that fateful night.

Other Notable Cases

Beyond these three intriguing examples, potential UFO crash sites abound across North America and beyond. Others include:

- **Shag Harbor, Nova Scotia (1967):** A supposed underwater

incident involving a UFO.
- **Varginha, Brazil (1996):** An incident involving the purported recovery of alien creatures.
- **Socorro, New Mexico (1964):** Featuring an alien encounter rather than a crash, but still contributing to the narrative of unexplained phenomena.

As investigations continue into these unsolved mysteries, one fact remains clear: the fascination with UFO crash sites fuels a desire to uncover cosmic truths while revealing our insatiable curiosity about what lies beyond. These unresolved narratives captivate researchers, history buffs, and conspiracy theorists alike, prompting endless debates. Far from mere relics of the past, these tales resonate deeply, conjuring potent questions about our place in the universe and the possibilities that await discovery.

In a world teeming with information, the allure of the unknown beckons, inviting enthusiasts to delve deeper into the shadows where truth and myth intermingle, urging us to uncover the secrets that lie amid the stars and refuse to fade away into the night.

2.3 Government Involvement

The enigma surrounding UFO crash sites often raises more questions than answers, particularly when considering the extent of government involvement in the investigation and handling of these incidents. The relationship between governmental entities and unidentified flying objects has evolved through decades of secrecy, speculation, and occasional disclosure. This subchapter aims to unravel the complex layers of government engagement regarding UFO crash sites, analyzing historical events, military actions, and the ongoing ramifications of this covert relationship.

Historical Context

In the early years of the UFO phenomenon, significant crash incidents attracted attention and concern from various governmental bodies. Notably, the infamous Roswell incident in 1947 is often cited as a pivotal moment in this saga. Here's a brief overview of key events that illustrate government involvement:

- **1947 Roswell Incident**: Reports surfaced of a "flying disc" crash near Roswell, New Mexico. Initial military statements claimed it was a weather balloon, but later, reports indicated it was indeed a classified project known as Operation Mogul. This discrepancy sparked public skepticism and theories of cover-up.

- **Project Blue Book**: Established in 1952 by the U.S. Air Force, Project Blue Book sought to investigate UFO sightings and assess any potential threat they posed. The project collected thousands of reports, yet most were subsequently debunked or explained away, leading to a public perception of government dismissal rather than serious inquiry.

- **Kecksburg Incident (1965)**: A UFO allegedly crashed in Pennsylvania reported by a number of witnesses. Military personnel swiftly secured the area, and the event was quickly downplayed, resulting in confusion and speculation about what exactly was recovered.

These incidents established a precedent for government involvement that would set the stage for numerous conspiracy theories suggesting that agencies possess knowledge far beyond what they reveal to the public.

Investigative Agencies and Their Roles

Various government entities have taken interest in UFO phenomena, primarily through intelligence and military agencies. Their roles and responses to reports of crash sites often suggest systemic approaches to understanding and managing these occurrences.

- **Central Intelligence Agency (CIA):** The CIA has historically monitored UFO sightings in tandem with national security concerns. Declassified documents reveal interest in how these phenomena could relate to foreign adversaries' military capabilities.

- **Defense Intelligence Agency (DIA):** The DIA has been involved in analyzing unidentified aerial phenomena, with evidence suggesting surveillance of potential foreign technology disguised as UFOs.

- **Federal Bureau of Investigation (FBI):** The FBI has conducted investigations into UFO reports and associated sightings, often collaborating with other departments for intelligence gathering and analysis.

Confidentiality and Secrecy

The veil of secrecy surrounding UFO crash investigations has fueled speculation and conspiracy theories among UFO enthusiasts and researchers. Highlights of these secrecy elements include:

- **Restricted Access:** Many documents related to UFO investigations remain classified, which raises questions about what governments are truly hiding.

- **Black Projects:** It's speculated that recovered materials from UFO incidents may have been used in classified military projects, which perpetuates the notion of a cover-up involving advanced technology.

- **Witness Suppression**: There are numerous accounts of whistleblowers and witnesses being silenced, either through intimidation or other means, further deepening public mistrust.

Recent Developments

In recent years, the push for greater transparency has led to notable shifts in governmental attitudes. The establishment of the Unidentified Aerial Phenomena Task Force and Congressional hearings signify a potential turning point:

- **UAP Task Force**: Launched by the Department of Defense, this task force aims to investigate and understand UFOs reported by U.S. military personnel, revisiting old cases with newfound scrutiny.

- **Report Releases**: The 2021 release of a preliminary report provided insight into over 140 incidents that could not be easily explained, prompting increased dialogue surrounding past and future government investigations into UFOs.

- **Public Interest**: As interest in UFOs has surged among the general population, pressure on government transparency has also increased, driving a need for more answers regarding crash incidents and unidentified technologies.

Conclusion

The intricate tapestry of government involvement in UFO crash sites blends elements of investigation, secrecy, and newfound openness, revealing a complex narrative that continues to evolve. As climate changes in public perception and governmental policy come to light, the quest for the truth about what lies behind these mysterious crash sites may finally be heading toward a clearer horizon. This ongoing evolution holds the potential to reshape our understanding and acknowledge the decades of speculation that have defined UFO discourse in the past century. The stakes remain high for both enthusiasts and skeptics alike, as the truth, however elusive, compels us all to question the narratives we've long accepted.

Chapter 3: The Cash-Landrum Incident

3.1 The Burning Craft

The phenomenon of UFO crash sites has fascinated both amateur enthusiasts and professional researchers alike. Among the plethora of reported incidents, few stand out as vividly as the various accounts of burning crafts, suggestive of advanced technology meeting an unyielding force: Earth's atmosphere. One of the most compelling accounts comes from the Roswell incident in 1947, but there are several lesser-known events that deserve examination.

Eyewitness Accounts

The vivid descriptions of these burning crafts have often come from witnesses who have observed strange objects, emitting smoke, flame, and debris, descending rapidly to the ground. These testimonials provide critical insights into the nature of the crafts and potentially the beings associated with them. Below are some common themes from eyewitness accounts:

- **Bright Lights**: Many observers speak of a brilliant flash that pierces the night sky, often described as a "fireball" or "meteor."
- **Sound**: Accompanying these visuals are often unexplained noises—roaring sounds, like rushing wind or mechanical grinding, indicating a possible malfunction.

UFO CRASH SITES

- **Smoke Trails**: Trailing plumes of black smoke have been reported, suggesting that these crafts may have experienced catastrophic failures.
- **Heat**: Witnesses frequently describe a significant amount of heat radiating from the crash site, even from a distance, casting doubts about their origin.

Following the initial moments of a craft's descent, the aftermath can become a complex scene rife with implications.

The Aftermath of the Crash

When a UFO is reported to have crashed, the consequences are multifaceted. Earthlings are often left grappling with the wreckage—the physical remnants of the craft and any potentially non-Earthly materials that may have survived the destruction. Such encounters invariably lead to intense investigation and sometimes cover-up.

- **Government Response**: Often, military or governmental authorities rapidly mobilize to secure the site. This was notably seen in Roswell, where military personnel quickly moved to gather and conceal evidence, igniting conspiracy theories that refuse to die.

- **Site Security**: Following the vehicle's descent, security measures are put in place to prevent civilian access. Reports of armed personnel and barricades raise suspicions regarding what truly transpired.

- **Scientific Examination**: In some cases, scientists or specialists are dispatched to examine the wreckage. Claims of extraordinary materials, such as metals that defy known metallurgy, fuel speculation about otherworldly technology.

Infamous Cases

While the Roswell incident remains etched in the annals of UFO history, several lesser-known crashes evoke equal mystery:

1. **Kecksburg, Pennsylvania, 1965**: Residents reported a glowing object crashing in the woods. Some described it as resembling an acorn. Local authorities arrived, and the area was cordoned off. Eyewitnesses who approached the site spoke of strange symbols on the craft's surface.

2. **Shag Harbour, Nova Scotia, 1967**: A group of locals witnessed a craft plunging into Shag Harbour. Despite extensive searches, no wreckage was ever officially documented. Strangely, bright lights were noted in the water following its descent.

3. **The Cash-Landrum Incident, Texas, 1980**: A dramatic account involves two women who encountered a fiery object, followed by the appearance of military helicopters. The aftermath of their experience led to severe health issues, raising discussions about potential government involvement in deliberate exposure to hazardous materials.

Technological Considerations

Speculation surrounding the technology of these craft adds layers to the inquiry surrounding burning crafts. Various theories abound:

- **Anti-Gravity Propulsion**: Could the propulsion system have malfunctioned, leading to an error in trajectory and descent?
- **Inverted Energy Patterns**: Reports suggest that some crafts may utilize energy sources that are entirely alien to our current understanding; failures in these systems could result in catastrophic exposure, generating flames.

Conclusion

The mystery of burning crafts and their crash sites serves as a window into something much larger—our place in the universe and what it means to encounter life beyond our Earth. The increasing availability of information, coupled with the internet's ability to connect enthusiasts, means that inquiries into these incidents continue to evolve. As researchers sift through decades of history and folklore, one certainty remains: the pursuit of truth in these enigmatic encounters is far from over. The charred remnants may whisper stories of interstellar journeys and worlds unseen, leaving us to ponder not just what happened there, but what they imply for a future where we are no longer alone.

3.2 Health Consequences for Witnesses

The phenomenon of UFO crashes often sparks curiosity and speculation, but a lesser-known aspect revolves around the health consequences faced by witnesses. Those who have encountered UFO crash sites may experience a range of physical and psychological effects that can have long-term repercussions. While many accounts remain anecdotal, certain patterns emerge from the testimonies of individuals who found themselves face-to-face with unknown craft.

Physical Health Consequences

Witnesses who claim to have been near a UFO crash site have often reported physical ailments that they attribute to their experience. These issues are varied and may include:

- **Radiation Exposure**: In several high-profile cases, individuals near crash sites have reported symptoms akin to radiation sickness. Eyewitnesses of the Roswell incident, for example, noted unusual sensations, burns, and other symptoms after purportedly coming into contact with debris from the crash.

- **Skin Irritations and Burns**: Reports of skin conditions, such as rashes and burns, have surfaced in accounts from witnesses in proximity to UFO crash sites. These conditions are often described as mysterious and resistant to conventional treatments.

- **Respiratory Issues**: Some witnesses report experiencing immediate respiratory problems following their encounter. This may include coughing, wheezing, and other breathing difficulties, potentially linked to toxic substances that might have been released into the environment during a crash.

- **Neurological Effects**: There are accounts suggesting that individuals near crash sites have experienced neurological symptoms, such as headaches, dizziness, and even temporary paralysis. Studies suggest these may result from exposure to unusual electromagnetic fields or substances associated with speculative alien technology.

Psychological Health Consequences

The psychological impact on those witnessing a UFO crash can be significant and multifaceted. Individuals may confront the following mental health challenges:

- **Post-Traumatic Stress Disorder (PTSD)**: The abruptness and the nature of the encounter can lead to lasting fear and anxiety. Many witnesses report recurring nightmares, flashbacks, and a pervasive sense of unease surrounding the incident.

- **Social Isolation**: Due to stigma and judgment, witnesses often find themselves isolated from friends and family. The fear of being labeled as "crazy" or "delusional" can inhibit open discussions about their experiences, exacerbating feelings of loneliness and despair.

- **Cognitive Dissonance**: Many witnesses struggle to reconcile what they saw with their understanding of reality. This conflict can lead to confusion, paranoia, and a shift in perception about their own belief systems.

- **Heightened Paranoia**: The culture surrounding UFOs often breeds distrust toward government entities and mainstream media. Witnesses may become increasingly suspicious, believing they are being monitored or that there is a cover-up concerning their experience.

Long-Term Consequences

The health repercussions of witnessing a UFO crash can be long-lasting. For some, it may lead to a lifelong pursuit of truth, while others are plagued by uncertainty and fear. The long-term consequences may include:

- **Chronic Health Issues**: Witnesses afflicted by immediate health complications may develop chronic conditions that reduce their quality of life. Ongoing studies into veterans and other groups exposed to unusual phenomena have highlighted troubling patterns of health ailments.

- **Identity Change**: For some, witnessing a UFO crash leads to a profound transformation in self-identity and beliefs. This change can cause estrangement from prior relationships and communities, creating a void that can be difficult to fill.

- **Continued Surveillance or Harassment**: Some witnesses report ongoing encounters with government personnel or agencies following the incident. This can create a sense of being targeted or controlled, leading to heightened anxiety and ongoing mistrust.

Conclusion

While individual experiences around UFO crashes vary widely, the potential health consequences for witnesses, both physical and psychological, merit serious consideration. Their stories, intertwined with the saga of human interaction with the unknown, bring to light the complexities of such experiences. Continued research and open discourse can aid in better understanding these facets of UFO phenomena, bridging the gap between anecdotal evidence and scientific inquiry. What remains clear is that the aftermath of witnessing such extraordinary events surpasses mere curiosity—it can alter health, perception, and identity for those who have stood at the edge of an enigma, possibly adjacent to the truth.

3.3 Legal Battles and Claims

In the realm of UFO crash sites, legal battles and claims have emerged as a significant aspect of the narrative, often intertwining with government secrecy, personal lawsuits, and claims of ownership over purported alien artifacts. These legal disputes reveal the complex interplay between individual rights, government policies, and the often elusive nature of evidence surrounding UFO experiences.

One of the most notable legal battles in the UFO realm arose from the alleged crash of an extraterrestrial spacecraft near Roswell, New Mexico, in July 1947. Initially classified as a "flying disc" by the military, the incident was later rebranded as a weather balloon recovery. This sudden shift ignited skepticism among UFO enthusiasts and historians alike, raising questions about government transparency. The repercussions of this cover-up narrative have echoed through decades, leading researchers and witnesses to pursue legal avenues to uncover the truth.

Key Legal Cases and Their Impact

Several significant legal cases have sought to challenge government secrecy and recover documentation regarding UFO incidents. Here are a few illustrative examples:

- **The Ramey Memo Case (Roswell)**: In 1994, researchers including Kevin Randle filed Freedom of Information Act (FOIA) requests to obtain critical documents related to the Roswell incident. The requests were often met with government defenses citing national security.

- **The Disclosure Project**: Founded by Dr. Steven Greer, this initiative sought to bring forward eyewitness testimonies and to compel the government to disclose classified information related to UFOs. While it didn't lead to direct legal action, it significantly raised public awareness and placed pressure on legal institutions.

- **U.S. Air Force vs. Citizens**: Over the years, numerous private citizens and researchers have engaged in legal battles to access government records. Often, these cases faced dismissal based on the grounds of national security or the lack of sufficient evidence for any alleged extraterrestrial involvement.

Personal Claims and Ownership Disputes

Beyond government interactions, private citizens have also ventured into legal disputes over ownership of supposed crash artifacts. The most famous case involves several residents of Roswell who claimed possession of unusual debris after the initial crash. The debate surrounding ownership unfolded in several ways:

- **Artifacts from Roswell**: Some individuals claimed to have salvaged pieces of the wreckage, leading to legal claims over ownership. Courts, however, typically ruled in favor of the general public or the government, arguing that such artifacts belonged to the state due to their potentially hazardous nature.

- **Militarized Artifacts**: As military personnel or ex-military individuals began to authenticate artifacts, disputes arose over the legitimacy of these claims. Legal actions ensued primarily around who had rights to artifacts if they had been found on military land or classified as evidence.

Public Sector Accountability

Furthermore, legal battles have often centered around accountability in government communication with the public. The growing fringe of UFO analysis has propelled citizens to call for transparency regarding alleged UFO encounters and crash sites. Such public lawsuits have:

- **Promoted Legislative Action**: Some legal disputes have triggered congressional inquiry into UFO phenomena. In recent years, reports submitted to the U.S. Congress about unidentified aerial phenomena (UAP) have spurred renewed accountability.

- **Led to Advocacy Groups**: Groups like the Mutual UFO Network (MUFON) and the Center for the Study of Extraterrestrial Intelligence (CSETI) utilize legal avenues to push for greater openness, often lodging complaints and requests that pressure agencies to provide historical UFO data.

Challenges in Legal Precedents

Legal battles in the UFO sphere face numerous challenges, not the least of which includes establishing a clear legal framework. The absence of a defined legal definition for UFOs or extraterrestrial phenomena creates hurdles for claimants.

- **Lack of Jurisprudence**: Courts frequently dismiss cases that attempt to claim ownership of artifacts without clear evidence linking such items to a tangible extraterrestrial event, causing frustration among claimants.

- **Secrecy Laws**: Many legal complaints face barriers due to existing secrecy laws that protect national security information. This legal shield often leaves petitioners without recourse.

In summary, legal battles and claims surrounding UFO crash sites reveal a rich tapestry of contention and intrigue. From engaged citizens seeking to obtain information from shadowy government narratives to those claiming ownership over mysterious artifacts, these disputes are as layered as the stories about the incidents themselves. The intersection of personal claims, government accountability, and the complexities of the legal system highlights how deeply invested individuals remain in unraveling the truths behind these monumental events in our history.

Chapter 4: The Phoenix Lights

4.1 A Night of Unexplained Phenomena

On a crisp autumn night in 1947, as the last rays of sunlight surrendered to twilight, the small town of Roswell, New Mexico, became the backdrop for an event that would ignite decades of speculation and intrigue surrounding unidentified flying objects (UFOs). What began as a seemingly ordinary evening would morph into a night of unexplained phenomena, intertwining local lore, military secrecy, and the burgeoning field of ufology.

As the clock struck midnight, a series of unusual lights flickered in the sky. Witnesses reported seeing a bright object darting erratically, its luminescence pulsating in vibrant hues of blue, green, and red. This was not merely a case of shooting stars or atmospheric anomalies; local residents, including sheriff's deputies and military personnel, were soon entangled in a web of strange occurrences that would alter their lives forever.

Eyewitness Accounts

The accounts from that fateful night vary significantly, but several themes emerge consistently:

- **Object Appearance**: Witnesses described a metallic disc-like shape, unlike any known aircraft of the time.
- **Heightened Emotions**: Many reported feelings ranging from

awe to fear as the object hovered silently above the ground, emitting a low-frequency hum that resonated through their bones.
- **Sudden Disappearance**: Following its dazzling display, the object vanished without a trace, prompting frantic searches by local residents.

One notable witness, Mac Brazel, a rancher who had been investigating strange debris scattered across his land, became pivotal to the Roswell incident narrative. He stumbled upon metal fragments that exhibited properties unknown to any earthly materials, seemingly defying physics itself. Initially uninterested by the police, Brazel's curiosity was piqued when military officials arrived, seizing the debris and declaring it was a "flying disc."

The Military Response

The next day, the Roswell Army Air Field (RAAF) took charge, leading to an official press release declaring that the U.S. military had recovered a "flying disc." This announcement sent shockwaves through the country, kicking off a media frenzy. Yet, mere hours later, the narrative took a surprising twist. Officials quickly backtracked, claiming the object was a weather balloon, leading many to suspect a cover-up.

The swift change in story gave rise to rampant speculation regarding the government's involvement in suppressing the truth about UFOs. This left the public questioning:

- What had really crashed in the New Mexico desert?
- Was the military hiding evidence of extraterrestrial life?
- Were there other witnesses who also encountered the bizarre occurrences?

An Investigation Begins

In the wake of the incident, various amateur and professional investigators, driven by curiosity and a quest for truth, began to probe deeper into the events of that night. Their investigations were often met with secrecy, but some key areas were covered:

- **Local Testimonies**: Researchers gathered firsthand accounts from citizens who witnessed the crash and the military's subsequent activities, revealing a tapestry of fear, excitement, and confusion.
- **Forensic Analysis**: Fragments of metal reported by Brazel were examined, revealing properties distinct from earthly materials, which only heightened the mystery.
- **Government Documents**: Declassified files from various intelligence agencies have periodically become available, although many maintain significant redactions about UFO research, sustaining the belief that hidden truths still lurk beneath the surface.

The Lasting Impact on Society

The Roswell incident marked a pivotal moment in American culture, establishing a framework for future paranormal investigations. It fostered a generation of UFO enthusiasts and conspiracy theorists, forever changing how the public perceived the possibility of extraterrestrial life. The blend of narrative storytelling and investigative journalism has since continued to unearth layers of mythology and misunderstanding surrounding UFOs, confirming that what occurred on that autumn night resonated well beyond Roswell.

As these events unfolded, an undeniable question lingered in the air, one that has yet to be definitively answered:

What remains unexplained about that night, and how deeply does the enigma of UFOs penetrate our understanding of reality?

This night of unexplained phenomena continues to inspire research into UFO crash sites, revealing that humanity's curious nature transcends time and circumstance in the quest to unveil the secrets that lurk beyond our world.

4.2 Military Explanations versus Public Belief

As interest in UFO crash sites has grown over the decades, a prevailing tension has formed between military explanations and the beliefs held by the general public. This dual narrative is not just a product of folklore and myth; it reflects deeper questions about authority, transparency, and the search for truth in the face of competing stories.

The Military Narrative

Historically, military institutions have wielded a tremendous influence over UFO phenomena. Key events, such as the Roswell Incident of 1947, showcased how military responses shaped public perception. When a mysterious object crashed on a ranch near Roswell, New Mexico, the U.S. Army Air Forces initially claimed to have recovered a "flying disc." This assertion was quickly retracted in favor of an explanation attributing the crash to a weather balloon.

This swift reversal illustrates a critical aspect of the military's relationship with UFO narratives:

- **Control of Information**: The military often exercises strict control over information regarding unidentified flying objects. This secrecy serves both to manage public fear and to safeguard national security.
- **Denial and Disinformation**: Over the years, there have been numerous cases of denial where military officials have classified certain incidents as mundane or misreported, leading to suspicions of official disinformation.
- **Scientific Discourse**: The military's approach to UFO

phenomena often includes a scientific lens, focusing on identifying foreign technology, which shifts the narrative from extraterrestrial speculation to national security concerns.

The military's official stance often emphasizes down-to-earth explanations, which de-emphasizes the public's more fantastical interpretations.

The Public Belief System

Conversely, public belief in UFOs is rich and varied, steeped in both personal experiences and cultural narratives. Many UFO enthusiasts view crash sites as evidence of extraterrestrial visitation. This perspective flourishes in a milieu where skepticism towards government narratives is common.

Several key factors contribute to public belief:

- **Eyewitness Accounts**: Personal testimonies from individuals claiming to have encountered UFOs or seen crash sites form a backbone of belief. These reports are often colorful and detailed, feeding into the larger narrative of alien visitation.
- **Cultural Influences**: Movies, television shows, and literature often frame UFOs as vehicles piloted by extraterrestrials, thus crafting a captivating mythology. This cultural portrayal reinforces the notion that UFO crashes are not only plausible but likely.
- **Conspiracy Theories**: Public belief often intertwines with conspiracy theories. The idea that government secrecy hides "the truth" about extraterrestrial encounters feeds a narrative that is both gripping and persistent.
- **Triangulation of Experience**: For many enthusiasts, personal anecdotes from family, friends, or community members bolster their belief systems, creating an experiential

layer that official accounts fail to provide.

The Clash of Perspectives

The confluence of military explanations and public beliefs has led to a complex discourse that continues to fuel debates around UFO crash sites. While the military promotes rational explanations and national security justifications, many in the public find these narratives unconvincing.

Areas of Divergence:

1. **Nature of Evidence**:

Military: Typically points to tangible evidence (e.g., debris, aircraft specifications) and scientific evaluations.

Public: Often emphasizes anecdotal evidence and personal experiences that resonate on a human level.

2. **Purpose of Disclosure**:

Military: Advocates for controlled information access, primarily framed around national defense and risk avoidance.

Public: Craves transparency and believes that the truth about UFOs will ultimately affirm their suspicions of extraterrestrial contact.

3. **Cultural Context**:

Military: Engaged in risk management, pragmatism, and accountability.

Public: Driven by a sense of curiosity, wonder, and the desire for connection with a broader universe.

Bridging the Gap

Ultimately, the divide between military explanations and public belief offers a unique lens into societal fears and hopes. It reflects a broader dialogue about truth, belief, and the complexities of a world that remains, at times, difficult to navigate.

As researchers continue to investigate these phenomena, critical questions will persist:

- How can we reconcile these different worlds?
- What will future revelations about UFO crash sites reveal about our understanding of ourselves and the cosmos?

In a culture increasingly shaped by skepticism and a thirst for the unknown, UFO crash sites serve as a rich tapestry through which the clashing narratives of military authority and public fascination can be examined, questioned, and perhaps, one day, reconciled.

4.3 Lasting Impact on the UFO Community

The emergence of reported UFO crash sites has had a profound and lasting impact on the UFO community, shaping beliefs, fueling investigations, and influencing the narrative about extraterrestrial life. These alleged incidents, particularly the famous cases like Roswell in 1947, transformed public perception and incited curiosity that has persisted for decades. By exploring the enduring effects of these events, we can better understand the intricate relationship between UFO phenomena and societal psychology.

One of the critical ways UFO crash sites have affected the community is through the establishment of a shared mythology. This narrative comprises details that appear based on collective witness reports, government secrecy, and tantalizing theories. For many enthusiasts, these sites represent not merely pockets of historic curiosity but corners of active inquiry into humankind's relationship with the cosmos. This shared mythology fosters a sense of belonging among enthusiasts, drawing in diverse individuals who seek answers to common questions:

- **Are we alone in the universe?**
- **What is the nature of extraterrestrial life?**
- **What hidden truths are governments keeping from us?**

Secondly, the significance of UFO crash sites has acted as a catalyst for numerous investigative initiatives. From amateur researchers to professional teams, many have dedicated their lives to uncovering the truths behind these events. As a result, UFO crash sites have become focal points for UFO organizations, such as the Mutual UFO Network (MUFON) and the Center for the Study of Extraterrestrial Intelligence (CSETI), which promote research and documentation of these phenomena. These groups advocate for:

- **Field investigations** to gather evidence and witness accounts.
- **Historical research** to analyze the broader context of these events.
- **Public education** to demystify the science surrounding UFOs and promote open discussions.

Additionally, the financial implications of these crash site narratives cannot be overlooked. Local economies have benefited significantly from increased tourism surrounding famous sites like Roswell or Kecksburg. Annual festivals, conventions, and UFO-themed activities draw enthusiasts and researchers alike, encouraging local businesses to cater to this unique demographic. The economic impact includes:

- **Visitor centers** featuring information about UFO sightings and crash incidents.
- **Storefronts selling memorabilia** such as books, clothing, figurines, and artwork.
- **Tour services** offering guided visits to significant crash site locations.

The intellectual impact of UFO crash sites has also been noteworthy. The phenomenon has inspired various fields of study, including sociology, psychology, and even parapsychology. Scholars have begun analyzing the dynamics of belief systems, the significance of collective memory, and how these factors contribute to the UFO narrative. The exploration of these sites raises questions around:

- **Cognitive dissonance**: Why do some individuals continue to believe in UFO phenomena despite skepticism?
- **Media influence**: How do documentaries, articles, and fictional representations shape public perceptions of UFO crash sites?
- **Sociopolitical dimensions**: What does the cultural fascination with alien encounters reveal about contemporary societal anxieties?

Moreover, the impact of these sites resonates significantly within conspiracy theories. The interplay between government cover-ups and UFO crash narratives gives rise to various theories that have pervaded public consciousness. This environment of suspicion encourages individuals to consider speculative and investigative avenues within their pursuits, leading to a range of beliefs that maintain interest and intrigue in extraterrestrial life. Prominent theories surrounding crash sites include:

- **Reverse engineering**: Claims that governments possess alien technology from crashed crafts, leading to technological advancements.
- **Government collaborations**: Speculation that extraterrestrials have engaged with governmental military agencies for purposes unknown to the general public.
- **Whistleblower accounts**: Individuals who allege insider knowledge about these incidents, fueling public interest in uncovering classified information.

Finally, the ongoing discourse surrounding UFO crash sites has helped usher in an era of increased transparency and disclosure. As the public becomes more aware of and interested in UFO phenomena, some governments have felt pressured to address UFO sightings and incidents more openly. Recent releases of official documents and videos have reignited discussions and enabled researchers to investigate the truth surrounding these enduring mysteries.

In conclusion, the lasting impact of UFO crash sites on the UFO community is multi-faceted, weaving together a rich tapestry of myth, investigation, economy, scholarship, conspiracy, and emerging transparency. As the narrative continues to evolve, the significance of these sites ensures that questions will remain—driving inquiry and curiosity that will likely endure for generations to come.

Chapter 5: The Socorro Landing

5.1 The Witness: Lonnie Zamora

Lonnie Zamora was no ordinary witness. A skilled law enforcement officer from Socorro, New Mexico, Zamora's life took an unexpected turn on April 24, 1964, when he encountered something that would elevate him into the discussions surrounding UFO phenomena. As a patrolman, he was well-versed in observing details, a skill that would serve him remarkably well during the events that unfolded that spring afternoon.

The Event Unfolds

The day began like any other for Zamora—routine patrols and traffic stops filled the hours. However, this ordinary day quickly transformed when the officer heard a strange sound, a loud roar, that made him pull over to investigate. Locating the noise led him to an area just outside of Socorro where he discovered an unusual object emitting a bright light.

- **Date**: April 24, 1964
- **Location**: Near Socorro, New Mexico
- **Time**: Early afternoon
- **Weather conditions**: Clear skies, visibility unobstructed

As Zamora approached the object, he described it as being egg-shaped, approximately 15 feet in length, and standing about 5 feet tall.

It was silver or metallic in color, and there were no visible markings or features, save for two legs. The sight was startling, and more perplexing was the realization that the object's presence could not be easily explained away.

The Encounter

Initially, Zamora thought he was witnessing a possible accident involving a vehicle. However, as he drew nearer, he observed two figures clad in white coveralls near the craft. The beings were described as small, around 3 or 4 feet tall, and their features were obscured by the structure of the craft itself.

Describing the scene further, Zamora claimed that as he approached, he felt a sense of unease, accompanied by the roaring sound intensifying. Suddenly, without warning, the craft rose into the air, leaving him startled and confused. The event transpired within mere minutes, but the effects would linger for decades.

Physical Evidence

After witnessing the craft take off, Zamora returned to the station to report the incident. His account drew skepticism from some colleagues, but several key physical pieces of evidence corroborated Zamora's testimony:

- **Burn Marks**: The area surrounding where the object had been resting exhibited scorched earth, scorched vegetation, and impressions resembling landing gear.
- **Witness Accounts**: Multiple individuals in Socorro reported having seen the object flying away, lending credibility to Zamora's testimony.
- **Local Examination**: Investigators from the U.S. Air Force's Project Blue Book visited the site shortly after, documenting the area and observing the remaining scorched patches.

Unpacking the Legacy

Zamora's account quickly became one of the most credible and discussed UFO sightings in history, providing researchers and enthusiasts with a wealth of information to analyze. The event invited several levels of scrutiny and interpretation: Was it a government experiment? A visitation from extraterrestrial beings? Or could it merely be an elaborate hoax?

Despite thorough investigations, no definitive conclusion was reached, but Zamora continued to stand by his experience. He maintained the honesty and integrity that characterized his law enforcement career, insisting he had witnessed something extraordinary.

The Impact

Lonnie Zamora's encounter had several ramifications:

- **Credibility in UFO Research**: Zamora's position as a police officer and his unwavering honesty lent significant weight to UFO research, urging further investigations.
- **Societal Impact**: This sighting engaged the public imagination about extraterrestrial phenomena, encouraging discussions and speculation that continue to this day.
- **Cultural Significance**: Zamora became somewhat of a folk hero among UFO enthusiasts, elevating the significance of the Socorro case in UFO lore.

In the years since the event, Zamora has become a symbol of credibility amid a swirl of skeptics and true believers alike, embodying the longing for answers in a universe filled with mysteries. Indeed, his experience continues to resonate, eliciting new investigations and theories about what lay at the intersection of science, myth, and the unknown. As we explore the broader topic of UFO crash sites, Zamora's encounter remains a pivotal moment in our understanding of humanity's relationship with the unexplained.

5.2 Analysis of Physical Evidence

UFO crash sites have long been the crux of numerous investigations by both amateur enthusiasts and professional researchers. The analysis of physical evidence from these sites often reveals intriguing insights into the events surrounding the purported crashes and the technologies involved. This subchapter delves into the types of evidence collected at UFO crash sites, the methodology employed in their analysis, and the implications that arise from these findings.

Types of Physical Evidence

When it comes to investigating UFO crash sites, the physical evidence can be broadly categorized into several types:

- **Material Evidence:** Fragments of metal, plastics, or unknown substances that do not match known earthly materials.
- **Geological Evidence:** Anomalies in the soil structure, alterations in the ground composition, or changes in local flora and fauna.
- **Radiological Evidence:** The detection of radiation levels that exceed natural background radiation, which might indicate either advanced technology or leftover energy from an unidentified source.
- **Witness Testimonies:** Eyewitness accounts that can provide context surrounding the crash and may lead to the discovery of other evidence.
- **Photographs and Videos:** Visual media documenting the scene, which can help corroborate or question the existence of physical evidence.

Methodologies Used in Analysis

Analyzing the physical evidence at UFO crash sites requires a multidisciplinary approach, combining techniques from the fields of archaeology, forensic science, materials science, and environmental studies. Some common methodologies include:

1. **Field Investigations:**

Initial Site Assessment: Documenting the geographical features, access points, and any potential disturbances to the crash area.

Photography and Videography: Capturing high-resolution images and videos of the site for further analysis.

Sample Collection: Carefully collecting materials from the site while maintaining the integrity of the samples.

2. **Laboratory Analysis:**

Materials Testing: Using methods like spectroscopy and chemical analysis to characterize the collected materials and determine their composition.

Radiation Testing: Employing Geiger counters and spectrometers to measure radiation levels in soil and debris.

Historical Research: Cross-referencing physical evidence with historical records to draw parallels and gain insight into the events surrounding the crash.

3. **Forensic Analysis:**

Chain of Custody: Ensuring that the evidence is handled properly to maintain its validity for analysis.

Comparative Analysis: Contrasting the findings with known terrestrial materials and technologies to assess anomalies.

Case Studies and Noteworthy Findings

Numerous crash sites have been reported throughout history, with some cases yielding particularly compelling physical evidence. Here are a few notable examples:

- **Roswell, New Mexico (1947):** Perhaps the most famous UFO incident, the Roswell crash allegedly produced metallic

debris that witnesses claimed was unlike any earthly material. Some pieces displayed unusual properties, such as being extraordinarily lightweight and resistant to bending.
- **Kecksburg, Pennsylvania (1965):** Witnesses reported a fireball in the sky, followed by the discovery of a metallic acorn-shaped object in the woods. Analysis of soil samples collected at the site revealed unusual deposits that some speculated could be remnants of the object.
- **Rendlesham Forest, England (1980):** British military personnel claimed to have encountered a craft emitting strange light and energy. Investigators later found depressions in the soil that indicated an unexplained force impacting the ground.

Implications of Findings

The analysis of these physical evidences has far-reaching implications, both scientifically and sociologically. Here are several key considerations:

- **Technological Advancements:** Discoveries of materials and technologies that defy known scientific explanations prompt questions about our understanding of physics and engineering.
- **Government Transparency:** Physical evidence frequently leads to discussions about governmental involvement, secrecy, and the potential cover-ups surrounding UFO incidents.
- **Public Perception:** The way physical evidence is presented and analyzed affects societal acceptance of UFO phenomena, often polarizing opinions between skeptics and believers.

In conclusion, the rigorous examination of physical evidence from UFO crash sites provides a compelling lens through which to explore the complexities of unidentified aerial phenomena. By employing scientific methodologies and integrating historical context, researchers continue to uncover narratives that may reshape our understanding of our world and the universe beyond.

5.3 Investigative Findings

The investigation into UFO crash sites often yields a complex tapestry of findings that intertwine the extraordinary with the mundane. In this chapter, we delve into the layers of evidence, witness testimonies, government responses, and the cultural impact of such incidents, all of which offer a nuanced perspective on our understanding of unidentified flying objects.

Historical Context

The allure of UFO crash sites gained momentum particularly after the Roswell incident of 1947. What initially appeared as a military intelligence cover-up blossomed into extensive conspiracy theories about government involvement in extraterrestrial affairs. With Roswell as a catalyst, a number of similar incidents across the globe have garnered attention.

Some notable cases include:

- **Kecksburg, Pennsylvania (1965):** Witnesses reported a fireball streaking across the sky, followed by military activity and a mysterious object being recovered.
- **Val Johnson Incident (1979):** Deputy Sheriff Val Johnson encountered an unknown object that allegedly caused damage to his patrol vehicle. This incident raised questions regarding the physical impacts of UFO encounters.
- **The 1980 Rendlesham Forest Incident:** Often described as Britain's Roswell, this event involved multiple military personnel witnessing strange lights and experiencing unexplained phenomena over several nights.

Each of these cases reflects a broader pattern of encounters that evoke curiosity and skepticism alike. What makes them compelling is not merely the sightings themselves but the responses and investigations that followed.

Physical Evidence

One of the core aspects of investigating UFO crash sites is the examination of physical evidence. Reports frequently mention unusual materials that defy conventional understanding. Investigators have noted:

- **Strange Metals:** Witnesses and investigators often describe metallic debris that exhibits properties unlike any terrestrial materials known. For instance, some crash sites revealed shards that levitated or had anomalous thermal properties.
- **Radiation Levels:** Certain crash sites, such as the one near Pine Bush, New York, recorded elevated radiation levels, raising questions about the craft's propulsion system and its potential effects on the environment and witnesses.
- **Unexplained Markings:** Land disturbances such as circular burn marks or imprints are common in reports, suggesting something left the ground differently than conventional aircraft.

Challenges in Verification

The challenge lies not only in the recovery of these materials but also in verifying their origins. Many findings are dismissed as mundane objects or natural phenomena. Furthermore, governmental secrecy and restrictions on investigations create barriers to conclusive evidence. This has given rise to speculation and theories regarding what remains undisclosed.

Witness Testimonies

Crucially, first-hand accounts play a vital role in the investigation of UFO crashes. Eyewitnesses can provide gripping narratives that serve to anchor the more abstract elements of evidence:

- **Credibility of Witnesses:** Many credible professionals, including military personnel, pilots, and scientists, have come forward with their own experiences, lending weight to the accounts of UFO crashes. Their proximity to these events often lends a degree of authenticity that is difficult to dismiss.
- **Emotional Impact:** Witnesses often describe profound psychological effects following their encounters, suggesting that these experiences extend beyond mere observation to involve a deeper existential impact.

Government Responses

The engagement of government agencies adds another layer of complexity to the investigation of UFO crash sites. Notably, the U.S. government's fluctuating stance on UFOs—from initial denial to eventual acknowledgment—has fueled public intrigue and speculation.

Key aspects of government response include:

- **Project Blue Book:** This was one of the most well-known investigations of UFOs, analyzing thousands of sightings between 1952 and 1969. Although the project concluded that most sightings were explainable, it also confirmed the existence of peculiar cases that defied logic.
- **Current Disclosures:** As of recent years, increased transparency surrounding UFO reports has sparked new public interest. The Pentagon's release of videos showing unexplained aerial phenomena has reignited theories around crash sites and military knowledge of extraterrestrial technology.

Cultural Impact

Finally, the ramifications of UFO crash investigations extend beyond empirical findings. They incite a playground of speculation, artistry, and intellectual debate. Cultural phenomena, ranging from literature to film, continue to explore the themes of extraterrestrial encounters and their implications on humanity's understanding of the universe.

In conclusion, the investigative findings surrounding UFO crash sites are multifaceted, comprising historical context, physical evidence, witness accounts, governmental responses, and cultural interpretations. These elements form a comprehensive narrative that captivates and challenges our understanding of reality, inviting enthusiasts and skeptics to ponder the great mysteries that linger in our skies.

Chapter 6: Roswell's Continued Legacy

6.1 Influence on Pop Culture

The intrigue surrounding UFO crash sites has seeped profoundly into popular culture, affecting everything from literature and film to television and music. The mythos surrounding these supposed extraterrestrial incidents not only captivates but also invites skepticism and speculation. As cultural artifacts, UFO crash sites have become fundamental elements in the broader narrative of human interaction with the unknown.

Literature: The Written Word and the Unknown

Books on UFO crash sites extend beyond mere accounts; they often weave tales of government cover-ups, alien technology, and secret military operations. Authors like Whitley Strieber with Communion and Charles Fort with Lo!, have built compelling narratives around these phenomena. These texts serve both as entertainment and as fodder for those seeking answers to unexplainable events.

Popular themes in this literature often include:

- **Government conspiracy**: Often reflecting contemporary fears about government transparency and accountability.
- **Alien life**: Explorations of what extraterrestrial beings could mean for humanity.

- **Mystery and resolution**: The tension between seeking proof of UFOs and the elusive nature of truth.

Film: The Silver Screen's Allure

Hollywood has long embraced the narrative potential of UFO crash sites, transforming real-life reports into thrilling, entertaining stories. Films like Close Encounters of the Third Kind and Independence Day are quintessential examples, blending science fiction with suspense and wonder about the unknown.

Key elements commonly portrayed include:

- **Government cover-ups**: Such as Area 51 being portrayed as a secretive haven for extraterrestrial technology.
- **Alien interactions**: Films often depict humanity's first contact with advanced civilizations, either as benevolent or malevolent.
- **Crisis scenarios**: The concept of facing an alien threat is a prevalent theme, often skewing historical accounts into epic battles for survival.

Television: A Ongoing Fascination

Television series have also tapped into the allure of UFO crash sites. Iconic shows such as The X-Files explore government conspiracies, alien encounters, and the supernatural. The combination of investigative journalism and the supernatural creates an addictive narrative.

Some notable trends include:

- **Paranormal investigation**: Series like Ghost Hunters delve into realms just beyond the visible, often referencing UFO sites.
- **Mini-series and documentaries**: Shows like Unsolved Mysteries or Ancient Aliens frame historical events in a

UFO-centric context, attracting audiences with mixed evidence and imaginative theories.

Music: Sounds from Beyond

The impact of UFO crash narratives can be heard in the music of various genres. Artists express their fascination and fear of the unknown through lyrical content and thematic music videos. Songs referencing UFOs resonate with those compelled by the mysteries of the universe.

Key artists and genres that have explored UFO themes include:

- **Classic rock**: Bands like Blue Öyster Cult and their hit (Don't Fear) The Reaper often reference existential themes, and UFO encounters.
- **Hip-hop**: Artists such as Janelle Monáe have incorporated UFO imagery and concepts in their work to critique society and identity.

Video Games: Interactivity with the Unknown

In the realm of gaming, UFO crash sites have provided a backdrop for adventurous plots and thrilling narratives. Titles like XCOM and No Man's Sky incorporate aliens and UFO phenomena, allowing players to explore the mysteries of the cosmos and engage with these concepts actively.

Common threads in video games include:

- **Exploration**: Offering players the chance to uncover unknown locations and interact with extraterrestrial beings.
- **Strategy and combat**: Engage in scenarios where players must confront or evade alien threats, often paralleling real-

world fears.

The Impact of UFO Culture on Society

The influence of UFO crash sites on popular culture reflects deeper societal beliefs and anxieties. The themes often echo:

- **Fear of the unknown**: Humanity's enduring curiosity about what exists beyond Earth.
- **Paranoia regarding authority**: Distrust in governmental bodies is echoed in narratives that depict cover-ups and secrecy.
- **Connection to existential questions**: Art and media serve as platforms for discussing broader issues about life, existence, and humanity's place in the universe.

In conclusion, the intersection of UFO crash sites and pop culture has shaped public perception and discourse. Whether serving as entertainment or a vehicle for deeper inquiry, these narratives reflect shared human curiosity about the mysterious world around us, ensuring that the allure of the unknown continues to captivate audiences across generations.

6.2 Books, Films, and Documentaries

The intrigue surrounding UFO crash sites has sparked a wealth of literature and media that delve into these mysterious events. From classic narratives to modern documentaries, the way these stories are presented can shape public perception and fuel further speculation. In this section, we will explore some of the most notable books, films, and documentaries that have contributed to the discourse on UFO crash sites, examining their impact on both popular culture and historical understanding.

Books

Numerous authors have sought to uncover the truth behind alleged UFO crash sites through detailed investigations, interviews, and analysis. Some pivotal works include:

- **"The Roswell Incident" by Charles Berlitz and William L. Moore**: This seminal book sparked public interest in the Roswell crash of 1947, documenting eyewitness accounts and suggesting a government cover-up. Berlitz and Moore's intriguing narrative helped fuel decades of speculation and investigation into other crash sites.

- **"UFO Crash at Roswell" by Kevin D. Randle and Donald R. Schmitt**: This work not only revisits the Roswell incident but also brings forth new evidence and testimonies, challenging previous interpretations. Randle and Schmitt's rigorous research has become a cornerstone of UFO literature.

- **"Crash: When UFOs Fall from the Sky" by Kevin Randle and others**: This comprehensive book recounts a range of alleged UFO crashes across the globe, synthesizing multiple sources and perspectives. The authors dive deep into incidents, examining both the stories themselves and the sociopolitical contexts in which they arose.

- **"Witness to Roswell: Unmasking the 60-year Cover-Up" by Thomas J. Carey and Donald R. Schmitt**: This volume features firsthand accounts from witnesses to the Roswell crash, providing compelling narratives drawn from interviews and archival research. It adds layers of complexity to the already rich Roswell lore.

Films

Cinematic portrayals of UFO crash sites dramatically highlight public fascination, blending eyewitness testimony with speculative dramatizations. Several films and docu-series stand out in this realm:

- **"Roswell" (1994)**: This TV miniseries dramatizes the Roswell incident and the surrounding conspiracy theories, captivating audiences with its blend of fact and fiction. While some criticize its accuracy, it undeniably helped popularize the narrative surrounding UFO crashes.

- **"The Day the Earth Stood Still" (1951)**: Though more a science fiction film, it reflects the era's anxieties surrounding alien visitation and the possible consequences. The underlying themes of alien encounters tie in with the discussions of crash sites.

- **"Unacknowledged" (2017)**: This documentary by Steven M. Greer explores alleged government cover-ups and features testimonies from individuals claiming encounters with extraterrestrial crafts. It offers a sensational yet thought-provoking perspective on the implications of UFO crash sites.

- **"The Phenomenon" (2020)**: This documentary explores the history of UFO sightings and encounters, including alleged crashes and their aftermath, prompting viewers to question what lies beyond the veil of government secrecy.

Documentaries

In addition to films, a number of documentaries have dedicated themselves to exploring specific events or broader themes related to UFO crash sites:

- **"UFO: The Truth Revealed" (2007)**: This documentary probes various UFO incidents, including crash sites, featuring interviews with reputed researchers and eyewitnesses. It serves as both an introduction to the subject and a deep dive for aficionados.

- **"Ancient Aliens" series**: While encompassing a broad array of themes, some episodes focus on reported UFO crash sites across history. The series connects historical events and artifacts to modern-day UFO phenomena, though with a mix of skepticism and acceptance.

- **"Out of the Blue" (2003)**: This documentary offers an overview of U.S. government involvement in UFO investigations and includes segments on crash sites, advocating for transparency and further research.

Conclusion

The literature and media surrounding UFO crash sites serve to fuel both fascination and skepticism. From books that critically analyze evidence to films that interpolate dramatized narratives with supposed truth, these resources have shaped our understanding of mysterious events throughout history. By engaging with these various narratives, enthusiasts and researchers can better navigate the complex landscape of UFO phenomena, distinguishing between credible investigations and sensationalist claims.

As the quest for truth continues, these works remain crucial in fostering discussion and stimulating further inquiry into what might lie behind the ongoing enigma of UFO crashes. Whether you are a steadfast believer, a curious skeptic, or a passionate researcher, the contributions of these authors and filmmakers play a pivotal role in marking the path toward greater understanding of our extraterrestrial curiosities.

6.3 Modern Conspiracy Theories

The landscape of UFO crash sites is littered with enigmas, where speculation collides with a fascination extending beyond mere sightings. Modern conspiracy theories regarding these sites provide a rich tapestry woven with half-truths, misinterpretations, and genuine mysteries. This subchapter delves into contemporary conspiracy theories surrounding notable UFO crash sites, illustrating how they have evolved alongside historical events and ballooned into a cultural phenomenon.

One of the most famous crash sites, located in Roswell, New Mexico, became a flashpoint for conspiracy theories. The 1947 incident, which involved the recovery of debris from an unidentified object, was initially reported by the military as a "flying disc." However, the U.S. government quickly changed its narrative, claiming the debris was linked to a weather balloon. This abrupt shift sparked a plethora of theories that have persisted for decades. Key conspiracy theories surrounding the Roswell incident include:

- **Alien Bodies Recovered:** Some proponents suggest that not only did the military recover a crashed craft, but also the bodies of extraterrestrial beings, which were allegedly stored in a secret facility for research.

- **Government Cover-Up:** A prevalent theory posits that the U.S. government actively concealed evidence of extraterrestrial life to prevent public panic, igniting deep mistrust among citizens towards government narratives.

- **Reverse Engineering:** Another conspiracy suggests that the technology from the Roswell craft has been reverse-engineered, leading to advanced military technologies and possibly influencing modern tech developments.

Beyond Roswell, other locations have garnered attention and inspired similar theories, though some may be less well-known. Notable among these sites are:

- **Kecksburg, Pennsylvania (1965):** Following a fireball sighting, a mysterious acorn-shaped object allegedly crashed in the woods. Witnesses claimed military personnel quickly cordoned off the area, fueling theories that the object contained alien technology.

- **Phoenix Lights (1997):** This event—where thousands reported seeing a massive, V-shaped craft—has led some theorists to assert that the lights were part of a military experiment or a cover-up of an alien visitation.

- **The Cash-Landrum Incident (1980):** In Texas, two women reported a close encounter with an unidentified flying object, which some theorists allege was related to an experimental government craft, leading to health issues from possible radiation exposure.

A pattern emerges with these theories: government secrecy breeds distrust and speculation, allowing UFO enthusiasts to connect apparent dots between events, military operations, and extraterrestrial encounters.

Moreover, the modern conspiracy landscape is heavily influenced by the internet and social media. The rapid spread of information—be it accurate, distorted, or entirely fabricated—has allowed conspiracy theories to proliferate at an unprecedented rate. Online platforms serve as breeding grounds where theories can gain momentum, often blending facts, hearsay, and conjecture. Consider the following aspects that enable this phenomenon:

- **Viral Media:** Videos, documentaries, and online forums facilitate discussions that can reach millions, often elevating fringe theories to mainstream conversations.

- **Echo Chambers:** Like-minded individuals create communities that reinforce existing beliefs, creating a feedback loop that can escalate conspiracy theories.

- **Documented Leaks:** Occasional government leaks and declassifications can lend credence to conspiracy theories, creating a sense that there are still secrets waiting to be uncovered.

Importantly, the allure of these conspiracy theories extends beyond the mere quest for truth. Debates around UFO crash sites tap into broader anxieties about technology, government transparency, and the unknown. Following historical moments marked by secrecy or intrigue—like the Cold War era—people have increasingly sought answers beyond what is publicly acknowledged.

As we navigate through these layers of modern conspiracy theories, it's essential to maintain a discerning eye. While many narratives can be dismissed as unsubstantiated or exaggerated, the intrigue surrounding UFO crash sites encourages inquiry into human experiences, government oversight, and the possibility of life beyond our planet.

The ongoing fascination with these sites is a reflection of humanity's innate desire to explore the unknown and question the narratives we are fed. Ultimately, in the world of UFO crash sites, the truth may be elusive, but the stories we create in our search for understanding reveal much about our society. The relevance of pondering these unexplained events continues to exist—after all, in a universe filled with mysteries, what we discover may be more illuminating than the answers themselves.

Chapter 7: Area 51 and Test Flights

7.1 The Mythos of Area 51

Area 51 has become synonymous with UFO sightings, alien conspiracies, and top-secret military operations in the popular imagination. Situated in the remote Nevada desert, this classified U.S. Air Force facility has been a fertile ground for speculation, folklore, and allegations of extraterrestrial encounters since its establishment in the 1950s. As UFO enthusiasts and conspiracy theorists delve deeper into the enigma surrounding this facility, the narratives often spin intricate tales that blur the lines between fact and fiction.

The mythos of Area 51 is heavily intertwined with various incidents and alleged crash sites attributed to UFO phenomena. The most credited of these is the Roswell incident of 1947, where reports of a "flying disc" emerged following a mysterious crash on a ranch in New Mexico. While the official explanation has always pointed to a weather balloon, believers argue that elements were later transported to Area 51 for study. This narrative paved the way for the facility's reputation as the epicenter of UFO-related activity.

Several factors contribute to Area 51's enigma:

- **Secrecy and Classification**: The U.S. government's longstanding silence about activities at Area 51 fuels speculation. Access to the base is highly restricted, with security measures that include military personnel, extensive surveillance, and no-fly zones. This veil of secrecy has led to rampant theories regarding what is really happening behind those fences.

- **High-Tech Aviation Testing**: While motivations are often obscured, Area 51 primarily serves as a testing ground for classified aircraft and advanced military technology. Projects like the U-2 and SR-71 Blackbird have taken flight here, further entrenching the notion that the government harbors advanced technologies that could be misconstrued as extraterrestrial.

- **Cultural Representation**: Area 51 has been depicted in films, television shows, and books, creating a lore that attracts curiosity and attention. From the alien-centric storylines of Hollywood blockbusters to documentaries investigating its secrets, the narrative has evolved into a significant aspect of modern folklore.

In the eyes of conspiracy theorists, Area 51 is not merely a military base; it embodies a microcosm of the hidden truths regarding UFOs and our understanding of outer space. Key incidents that contribute to its mythos include:

- **The Majestic 12 Document**: Alleged to be a secret committee formed in the aftermath of Roswell to study alien technology, this document has fueled speculation that the U.S. government is covering up vital information about extraterrestrial contacts.

- **Bob Lazar's Claims**: A self-proclaimed engineer who claimed to have worked on reverse-engineering alien spacecraft at Area 51, Lazar's assertions have captivated conspiracy circles. His detailed descriptions of technology and encounters with alien crafts have given birth to countless theories and discussions.

- **The Black Projects**: Many postulate that Area 51 is a site for experiments on crashed alien ships and the reverse-engineering of extraterrestrial technology. While the idea seems fantastical, it remains a popular belief among UFO enthusiasts.

As myths surrounding Area 51 deepen, stories of UFO crash sites also evolve, sparking interest in:

- **The Kecksburg Incident**: This lesser-known event involved a bell-shaped craft that allegedly crashed in Pennsylvania in 1965. Witnesses reported a recovery operation by military personnel reminiscent of other UFO incidents, linking its narrative to the secrecy of Area 51.

- **The Phoenix Lights**: Witnessed by thousands in 1997, this mass sighting in Arizona raised questions about military exercises and unearthly craft, with many speculating connections to the activities at Area 51.

- **Socorro, New Mexico**: The 1964 sighting by police officer Lonnie Zamora included an encounter with a strange craft and otherworldly beings, further embedding Socorro into the interconnected web of UFO and Area 51 lore.

The mythos of Area 51 transcends mere conspiracy; it symbolizes humanity's quest to understand the unknown. As UFO crash sites become focal points for inquiry and analysis, Area 51 stands at the center—a labyrinth of secrecy, innovation, and the ever-elusive search for truth in our universe. The intrigue surrounding this facility continues to incite imagination, drawing in a diverse crowd of enthusiasts, researchers, and skeptics alike, all eager to unravel what lies beyond the veil of secrecy.

7.2 UFO Researcher Perspectives

UFO research has evolved significantly since the early 20th century, with many researchers dedicating their lives to uncovering the truth behind unidentified flying objects and alleged crash sites. Each researcher brings their unique lens to this captivating topic—some grounded in scientific inquiry, while others are influenced by personal experiences or social contexts. This section explores the perspectives of several prominent UFO researchers and their approaches to investigating crash sites.

The Pragmatic Investigator

One category of UFO researchers approaches the subject with a pragmatic mindset. They draw on scientific methods, rigorous data collection, and clear investigative frameworks. These researchers often advocate for transparency, urging governments to release classified information regarding UFO sightings and incidents.

Key Attributes:

- Emphasis on empirical evidence
- Use of scientific methodologies
- Advocacy for governmental transparency

Dr. Richard Haines, a former NASA scientist, is a prominent figure in this category. Haines has extensively analyzed eyewitness reports, particularly those related to UFO sighting patterns, and has also investigated claims of crashed UFOs. His studies lead him to posit that these objects exhibit technological capabilities far beyond current human technologies, leading many to wonder just what lies within the government archives. Haines' work highlights the necessity of scrutinizing photographs, eyewitness accounts, and particularly vexing government documents.

The Historical Scholar

Another group comprises historians and archivists who contextualize UFO incidents within larger historical narratives. They understand that modern UFO phenomena didn't start in a vacuum; they are intertwined with the sociopolitical climate, advancements in aviation, and the cultural zeitgeist of their specific eras.

Areas of Focus:

- Historical narratives surrounding UFOs
- The influence of media on public perception
- Document analysis from different time periods

Dr. David Clarke, a British ufologist and historian, investigates these intersections. His work sheds light on how public interest in UFOs surged during the Cold War, amidst fears of espionage and technological advancement. His analyses of declassified documents provide insights into both military responses to reported sightings and civil society's reaction to these narratives. Clarke emphasizes the importance of analyzing cultural artifacts such as films and literature, which reflect and shape public attitudes toward UFOs.

The Contactee Perspective

Not all researchers come from academic or scientific backgrounds. Some are self-proclaimed "contactees" and investigate crash sites from a personal experience approach. These researchers focus on their own narratives or those of others who claim to have had encounters with extraterrestrial beings.

Key Themes in Research:

- Personal testimonies and abduction experiences
- Psychological and emotional impacts of encounters

- Community-building among contactees

One influential figure in this realm is Dr. Barbara Lamb, who has conducted extensive interviews with individuals claiming encounters with extraterrestrials. Lamb's research emphasizes the profound emotional and psychological effects of these experiences, as well as their implications for understanding humanity's place in the cosmos. Her perspective challenges the purely empirical approach, asserting that the subjective, personal aspects of these encounters are also valuable data worthy of investigation.

The Skeptical Analyst

The skeptics play a crucial role in the UFO crash site discourse. They raise essential questions about the motives behind claims and challenge the veracity of evidence presented by proponents of alien crash narratives.

Common Skeptic Arguments:

- Lack of reproducible evidence
- Psychological explanations for sightings
- Cultural influences on reporting and interpretation

One notable skeptical researcher is Dr. Michael Shermer, a well-respected science historian and founder of the Skeptics Society. He focuses on investigating claims of extraordinary phenomena using critical thinking and the scientific method while challenging the tendency of people to jump to conclusions without adequate evidence. Shermer has been vocal about the need for rigorous standards in both UFO research and the interpretation of reported incidents.

Conclusion

The discourse surrounding UFO crash sites is enriched by the diverse perspectives of researchers from various backgrounds. Together, they form a mosaic of inquiry that captures the complexities of this enigmatic subject. Each perspective, whether pragmatic, historical, experiential, or skeptical, adds to our understanding of UFO phenomena. As we delve deeper into the mysteries of these alleged crash sites, it becomes increasingly clear that the search for truth in the realm of UFOs requires an interdisciplinary approach.

The investigation of UFO crash sites not only invites speculation about extraterrestrial life but also compels us to reflect on our history, beliefs, and the very nature of evidence itself. As researchers continue to sift through the layers of evidence, personal stories, and historical context, the search for knowledge becomes as compelling as the mystery itself.

7.3 Legitimizing the Legends

The investigation into UFO crash sites has often been overshadowed by skepticism and urban legend. Yet, as more accounts surface and historical analyses emerge, there is a growing need to distinguish between myth and reality. This journey of legitimizing the legends not only involves sifting through anecdotal evidence but also understanding the cultural and governmental contexts that have contributed to the lore surrounding these infamous locations.

The Birth of Legends

Many UFO crash site stories originated during the post-World War II era, a time marked by heightened public interest in extraterrestrial life. The Roswell incident in 1947 serves as a prime example of how a single event can burgeon into a sprawling network of conspiracy theories and folklore. Other noted incidents, such as the Kecksburg crash of 1965 and the crash near Corona, New Mexico, have similarly fueled speculation and prompted various interpretations.

The narratives surrounding these incidents often feature common motifs:

- **Military Secrecy**: Many crash sites are alleged to have been swiftly covered up by military authorities. Reports of unmarked black vehicles and armed personnel appear regularly in eyewitness testimonies, lending an air of credibility to claims of concealed alien technology.

- **Extraterrestrial Materials**: Eyewitnesses frequently describe strange materials recovered from the crash sites—metals that are lightweight yet incredibly strong, or substances that appear to behave contrary to known physical laws.
- **Witness Testimonies**: Accounts from military officials, civilians, and even alleged whistleblowers add layers of intrigue. These testimonies either support or contradict the official narratives, contributing to the tapestry of legend surrounding these crash sites.

Unraveling the Mysteries

While an examination of these legends may invite skepticism, the persistence of certain stories signals the potential for truth beneath the surface. To legitimize the legends of UFO crash sites, researchers employ a multi-faceted approach, focusing on several key elements:

1. **Historical Context**: Analyzing the sociopolitical climate at the time of alleged incidents often reveals motivations behind public interest and media coverage.

2. **Government Documentation**: Official records, such as military reports and declassified documents, provide a framework through which claims can be validated or dismissed.

3. **Correlation with Technological Advances**: Emerging technologies from the era—like radar technology, advances in propulsion systems, and burgeoning interest in rocketry—become critical points of discussion in potential alien technology discussions.

4. **Scientific Inquiry**: Engaging with scientific communities can illuminate possibilities concerning the materials purportedly found at crash sites, fostering a more nuanced understanding of their origins.

Research and Investigation

To further legitimize the narratives surrounding UFO crash sites, there is a call for methodical investigation. Researchers and enthusiasts can participate in such inquiries through various means:

- **Field Investigations**: Engaging in on-site research can uncover physical evidence, such as geographical anomalies or debris that might corroborate eyewitness claims.
- **Archival Research**: Delving into newspapers, military archives, and personal accounts can reveal often-overlooked details that provide context to the legends.
- **Community Engagement**: Networking with local histories and gathering testimonies from those who experienced the events firsthand yields invaluable insights that can validate claims.

The Role of Technology and Media

In the digital age, the interplay between technology and media significantly contributes to the legitimization process. Investigations utilizing drone technology, for instance, can cover vast terrains where physical evidence remains hidden. Advanced analytics can assist in mapping historical accounts with geographical data, providing a clearer picture of where incidents occurred.

Furthermore, the dissemination of information through online platforms has enabled a community of UFO enthusiasts, historians, and researchers to unite in their quest for truth. Documentaries, podcasts, and interactive forums now serve as collaborative spaces where legends can be debated, dissected, and examined from various angles.

Conclusion

Legitimizing the legends of UFO crash sites involves navigating a complex maze of historical context, witness testimonies, and technological advancements. By incorporating rigorous investigative practices and embracing an open-minded yet critical lens, the stories can transcend mere folklore to reveal deeper truths about our interaction with the unknown. Embracing both skepticism and curiosity is vital; exploration may uncover not only the remnants of unidentified flying objects but also the continuous human quest for understanding the mysteries of the universe. In a world where legends and truths intertwine, every inquiry brings us one step closer to illuminating the enigma of our skies.

Chapter 8: The Hudson Valley Sightings

8.1 A Decade of Reports

In the past decade, the phenomenon of UFO sightings and their alleged crash sites has captured the interest of researchers, historians, and enthusiasts all around the globe. As technology has advanced, so too has the means by which reports and evidence are documented. Each year, a steady stream of accounts emerges—some credible, others fueled by speculation—that contribute to an ever-growing tapestry of what many consider to be the most enduring mystery of our time.

From the revelation of government documents to the personal testimonies of witnesses, the last ten years have seen a marked increase in the analysis and disclosure of information regarding UFO crash sites. In particular, the intersection of declassified military files and civilian encounters has created a fertile ground for discussion, raising questions about what these incidents reveal about both our history and the potential existence of extraterrestrial life.

Key Incidents of the Decade

1. **The 2017 Pentagon UFO Revelations**: The release of videos by the Pentagon featuring unidentified aerial phenomena (UAP) sparked renewed interest in UFOs. These disclosures not only confirmed the government's acknowledgment of UFOs but also suggested that some may have crashed or come to the attention of military personnel due to anomalous behavior.

2. **The Roswell Report**: 70 years after the infamous Roswell incident in 1947, renewed interest surfaced with new interviews and investigations. Witnesses and alleged participants involved in the original recovery of debris came forward in greater numbers, some claiming to have seen extraterrestrial technology.

3. **The 2020 UAP Task Force**: A congressional report released in 2021, based on UAP sightings from military personnel, included discussions of unexplained aerial phenomena. This report stirred public intrigue about whether any of these phenomena were indicative of crash sites or remnants of alien technology.

4. **Individual Case Studies**: Various organizations, such as the Mutual UFO Network (MUFON) and the National UFO Reporting Center (NUFORC), documented numerous other reports from across the United States and globally. Notable crash-site claims included:

Kecksburg, Pennsylvania (1965): Witnesses reported a metallic object crashing in a wooded area. Army personnel allegedly recovered the object before civilians could reach the site.

Maury Island, Washington (1947): A report by Harold Dahl claimed that he saw six flying saucers, one of which crashed on his boat.

Growing Evidence and Technology

Over the last decade, technological advancements have significantly influenced how sighting reports are captured and analyzed. The integration of smartphone cameras, drones, and advanced imaging technologies has led to the emergence of clearer, more detailed footages of supposed UFOs or their crash sites. Citizen scientists using open-source data and forensic analysis techniques are increasingly taking the initiative to investigate these occurrences.

Moreover, Internet forums and social media platforms have acted as dissemination channels for witnesses to come forward. The capacity for citizens to share their accounts in real-time has created a more connected community, resulting in collaborative investigations that span across borders.

Challenges in Investigation

While the decade has provided exciting leads and testimonies, certain challenges persist when examining UFO crash reports. Key obstacles include:

- **Misinformation**: The sensational nature of some reports leads to considerable misinformation and "hoaxes," complicating the process of separating fact from fiction.
- **Government Secrecy**: The classifications surrounding military operations and potential recovery of crashed UFOs often inhibit thorough investigation and transparency.
- **Evolving Public Perception**: The general public's changing attitude toward UFOs—from ridicule to openness—can impact the willingness of witnesses to share their experience.

Conclusion

The last ten years of UFO crash site reports underscore a compelling narrative filled with intrigue, mystery, and the inexhaustible human quest for truth. As researchers continue to sift through a decade's worth of accounts, a more comprehensive understanding of these phenomena is gradually emerging. Whether grounded in fact or a shimmering lure of possibility, the quest for understanding UFOs and their alleged crash sites remains a riveting chapter in both historical inquiry and contemporary investigation.

In closing, as interest grows, public forums and governmental oversight may bear witness to an even deeper exploration of these reported incidents, hinting that the story behind UFOs—crash sites included—is far from over. The timeline leading from past occurrences to present-day inquiries and future revelations will likely shape our understanding of the universe and our place within it.

8.2 Explanations and Skepticism

The exploration of UFO crash sites has captivated public imagination for decades, igniting fervent debates among enthusiasts, skeptics, and researchers alike. While many people view these sites as evidence of extraterrestrial encounters, a more grounded perspective invites us to examine alternative explanations and the skepticism that surrounds various claims associated with these incidents.

At the core of the UFO crash phenomena lies the question: What truly happened at these locations? From the infamous Roswell incident of 1947 to lesser-known events scattered around the globe, the stories of crashed UFOs are often steeped in mystery. Yet, these tales thrive against a backdrop of counter-narratives and rational skepticism.

Alternative Explanations

Many skeptics argue that reports of UFO crashes can often be attributed to more terrestrial phenomena. Some of the most common alternative explanations include:

- **Military Testing**: During the post-World War II era, the world saw an upsurge in military activity related to experimental aircraft. Some incidents once labeled as UFO crashes were later revealed to be related to advanced military projects, such as the U-2 or the SR-71 spy planes.

- **Weather Balloons**: The infamous Roswell incident is frequently cited as a classic example of a misidentified military weather balloon. Although proponents of the extraterrestrial theory reject this explanation, the government has consistently stated that what the public encountered was indeed a weather balloon used for high-altitude research.

- **Astronomical Events**: Many UFO sightings, including purported crash events, can be linked to natural phenomena such as meteor showers or atmospheric anomalies that confuse witnesses. These incidents often serve as reminders that the human perception of the skies can be misleading.

- **Psychological Phenomena**: The power of suggestion, particularly in an era filled with media and cultural hype around UFOs, can lead individuals to misinterpret ordinary objects or events as otherworldly. Cases of pareidolia, where the mind sees familiar patterns, can also play a role in shaping these belief systems.

Cultural Context

The fascination with UFOs also reflects the socio-political climate of different eras. The Cold War spurred a wave of anxiety about the unknown, leading people to latch onto alien theories as a metaphor for fears regarding espionage and invasion:

- **Post-War Fear and Anxiety**: The societal backdrop of the late 1940s and 1950s, filled with uncertainty and the threat of nuclear annihilation, provided fertile ground for the emergence of UFO lore. Many people sought explanations for their growing fears, and extraterrestrial encounters became a lens through which they could reinterpret their realities.

- **Mythmaking**: As UFO crash sites gained notoriety, some elements of the narrative began resembling folklore and myth, with certain sites being romanticized — Roswell being the prime example but joined by claims from Kecksburg or the Rendlesham Forest incident.

Sifting Through the Claims

When evaluating the legitimacy of UFO crash site stories, a critical and analytical approach is crucial. Researchers often recommend several key methodologies:

- **Corroborative Evidence**: Always seek multiple sources to corroborate claims concerning UFO sightings or crashes. Peer-reviewed research or accounts from reputable investigative bodies can lend credibility to findings.

- **Examine Motives**: Consider the motives behind the witnesses or claims, ranging from personal experiences to financial gain through book deals or documentaries. Understanding the context can help distinguish genuine encounters from sensationalism.

- **Scientific Inquiry**: Rely on scientific methods to explore physical evidence, such as debris or materials reportedly retrieved from crash sites. Rigorous analysis can often dispel or affirm extraordinary claims.

Embracing Skepticism

Skepticism plays a vital role in any investigative pursuit, including UFO studies. Healthy skepticism fosters a culture where ideas can be challenged, tested, and ultimately refined. It empowers researchers and enthusiasts to discern truth from fabrication, reinforcing the notion that not every report of unusual phenomena merits belief.

Some notable critiques of the UFO narrative include:

- **Confirmation Bias**: Many enthusiasts may focus solely on information or events that support their beliefs while ignoring contrary evidence.

- **Lack of Empirical Validation**: UFO claims often rely on anecdotal evidence rather than rigorous scientific validation. Without physical proof, claims remain firmly in the realm of speculation.

In conclusion, as we delve into the anomalies surrounding UFO crash sites, an open yet skeptical mindset becomes our best tool. While the allure of the unexplained continues to draw us in, it is the analytical lens that will ultimately guide us toward a clearer understanding of what these incidents might truly signify in our quest for knowledge about extraterrestrial life.

8.3 Documenting the Evidence

As interest in UFO crash sites continues to burgeon, the need for rigorous and systematic documentation of evidence becomes ever more crucial. Documenting the evidence surrounding these enigmatic events not only provides a foundation for future investigative pursuits but also assists in substantiating claims made by witnesses, researchers, and enthusiasts alike. Whether addressing an alleged incident from decades past or a more recent occurrence, a meticulous approach to evidence gathering and documentation is essential.

The Importance of Documentation

The first step in understanding UFO crash sites involves acknowledging that each incident is steeped in a complex narrative. Accurate documentation helps to:

- Preserve the integrity of witness testimonies.
- Function as a historical record for future reference.
- Assist in correlating various reports, potential evidence, and subsequent analyses.
- Contribute to comprehensive databases that can be used by researchers globally.

Without systematic documentation, even the most compelling stories can languish in obscurity. Therefore, setting up protocols for collecting and documenting evidence is vital.

Types of Evidence to Document

The nature of UFO incidents can vary dramatically, and so too can the types of evidence that emerge. In approaching documentation, investigators may categorize evidence into the following categories:

1. **Physical Evidence**:

Metal fragments

Soil samples

Radiation readings

Burn marks or vegetation alterations

2. **Witness Testimonies**:

Eyewitness accounts detailing specific experiences

Descriptions of the craft, sounds, lights, and behaviors observed

Impacts on the community, such as reports of missing time or psychological effects

3. **Photography and Video**:

Images of the crash sites

Videos capturing the incident or immediate aftermath

Aerial photographs of the location for context

4. **Government or Military Disclosures**:

Official reports and documents

Communication records with any military authorities involved

Responses from FOIA (Freedom of Information Act) requests

5. **Scientific Analysis**:

Expert evaluations of physical evidence

Analysis of soil and atmospheric conditions at the time of the incident

Corroboration with known phenomena, such as meteorological data

Methodologies for Documenting Evidence

A critical aspect of thorough evidence documentation is developing robust methodologies that ensure the credibility and utility of the information gathered. Here are several methods to consider:

- **Field Research Protocols:**

Create detailed reports immediately after visiting the crash site.
Employ a photographic log, documenting every detail from multiple angles.
Calculate GPS coordinates to establish precise locations of anomalies.

- **Interviewing Witnesses:**

Use open-ended questions to encourage comprehensive narratives.
Record interviews (with permission) to capture verbal nuances and stress.
Cross-reference narratives based on timing, location, and descriptions.

- **Collating Documentation:**

Organize all materials chronologically, thematically, or by relevance.
Utilize digital platforms to create a database that allows for quick reference and updates.
Encourage sharing this information with wider databases and UFO research organizations.

- **Establishing a Chain of Custody:**

For any physical evidence, maintain a strict chain of custody to ensure authenticity.

Document who collected evidence, where it was stored, and how it was handled.

Evaluating and Analyzing the Evidence

Once evidence is documented, the next phase involves scrutiny and analysis. Researchers should strive to:

- Identify patterns and correlations across different incidents.
- Consult experts in relevant fields such as metallurgy, psychology, or environmental science.
- Share findings with other researchers and enthusiasts to foster collaborative investigations.

Conclusion

Documenting evidence from UFO crash sites is more than a prerequisite for validating claims; it is a vital practice that contributes to a broader understanding of unexplained phenomena. Through comprehensive documentation, researchers can piece together the fragmented narratives surrounding these incidents, revealing insights that may otherwise go unnoticed. As we continue to investigate these extraordinary events, we cannot underestimate the power of precise documentation to illuminate the dark corners of our world. Ultimately, it is through meticulous efforts to preserve and analyze evidence that we can hope to unravel the mysteries of UFO crash sites, fostering a community driven by inquiry and discovery.

Chapter 9: Band of Brothers: The Malmstrom Air Force Base Incident

9.1 Event Overview

The phenomenon of UFO crash sites has ignited a fervent interest among researchers, enthusiasts, and skeptics alike. These locations, often shrouded in secrecy and controversy, hold the promise of unraveling mysteries that transcend the boundaries of known science and conventional history.

Historically, the allure of UFO crash sites dates back to the mid-20th century, particularly with the emergence of the modern UFO phenomenon post-World War II. Perhaps the most infamous case that galvanizes interest in this realm is the Roswell Incident of 1947, where an alleged extraterrestrial craft purportedly crashed on a ranch in New Mexico. This singular event would set the groundwork for decades of speculation, investigation, and conspiracy theories surrounding government cover-ups and alien technology.

Key Features of UFO Crash Sites

UFO crash sites often share several characteristics that make them the focal point of investigations:

- **Mysterious Debris**: Eyewitnesses frequently describe unusual materials that are resistant to destruction, often contradictory to terrestrial aerospace engineering.

- **Witness Testimonies**: Many crash sites attract individuals who claim to have seen unexplained phenomena. These accounts typically highlight atmospheric anomalies, lights in the sky, or metallic objects behaving in ways that defy normal physics.
- **Government Involvement**: Reports of military presence shortly after an incident suggest a cover-up or a retrieval operation. These instances raise questions about what information is withheld from the public.
- **Radiation and Anomalies**: Some investigators note that several crash sites show elevated radiation levels or other environmental anomalies, leading to considerations about the technologies that might have been involved.

Historical Context

Understanding the context within which these incidents arise is crucial. The Cold War era, the dawn of the space race, and rising public interest in science fiction all contribute to the backdrop against which public interest in UFOs surged. High-profile government projects like Project Blue Book, and events such as the 1975 explosion of an alleged UFO in the Brazilian countryside, highlight the international implications and conspiracy rabbit holes that UFO crashes initiate.

Several notable crash sites provide insights into the historical narrative of UFO activity:

- **Roswell, New Mexico (1947)**: Often considered the cradle of modern UFO lore, its aftermath includes conflicting explanations from government officials, sparking lifelong interest.
- **Kecksburg, Pennsylvania (1965)**: Dubbed the "Kecksburg UFO Incident," a fireball was reported across several states, leading to eyewitness accounts of a metallic object and

subsequent military recovery efforts.
- **The Socorro Incident (1964)**: In Socorro, New Mexico, police officer Lonnie Zamora reported seeing a "bathtub-shaped" spacecraft and two small beings, which would later draw the scrutiny of various investigators.
- **Bariloche, Argentina (1995)**: This crash involved reports of a UFO in distress, gradually fading from sight and raising countless questions about its origin.

Investigative Techniques

Investigating UFO crash sites requires a unique approach that combines elements of forensics, history, and sometimes, speculative science. Techniques used in this field often include:

- **Field Investigations**: Conducting on-site analyses where eyewitness accounts were reported, collecting soil samples, or examining environmental factors.
- **Historical Document Review**: Scrutinizing military archives, government correspondence, and local media reports for any evidence of cover-ups or past incidents.
- **Interviews and Testimonies**: Engaging witness accounts through interviews helps assemble a narrative that could potentially piece together the unknown aspects of an event.

Community and Cultural Impact

UFO crash sites elicit not only investigative interest but also cultural significance. They often become pilgrimage sites for enthusiasts who seek to connect with something beyond the known. Documentaries, films, and books continually propagate these stories into mainstream culture, reinforcing the narrative that the skies may house more than what is comprehensible.

In conclusion, the exploration of UFO crash sites serves as a nexus between historical inquiry and the quest for knowledge beyond our earthly bounds. Each site tells its own story, inviting us to consider possibilities that extend far into the cosmos while simultaneously challenging entrenched certainties about our place in the universe. The ongoing fascination with these anomalies reveals more about human curiosity and the yearning to understand the unexplained than merely the incidents themselves.

9.2 Military Protocol and Reactions

In the aftermath of reported UFO crashes, military reactions have often been shrouded in secrecy, speculation, and an overwhelming sense of urgency. Understanding how various military branches have approached UFO crash sites reveals a fascinating intersection of protocol, public perception, and the unknown. Governments worldwide have been involved in these investigations, but the United States military's protocol has been the most scrutinized, primarily due to incidents like Roswell and the numerous sightings during the Cold War.

Initial Response

When a UFO crash is reported, the first responders typically include local law enforcement. However, as the situation escalates, the military often intervenes. The following steps outline the typical military protocol upon discovery of a UFO crash site:

- **Assessment of the Situation**: Initial reports are assessed for credibility. This involves gathering eyewitness statements and determining the location and nature of the object.
- **Securing the Area**: The military secures the crash site, establishing a perimeter to prevent civilian access. This action is crucial not only for protecting sensitive information but also for controlling the narrative surrounding the event.
- **Identification**: Reconnaissance teams are dispatched to

determine what kind of craft has crashed. This phase includes identifying materials, potential technology, and any biological evidence, should there be any living entities involved.

The Chain of Command

One significant aspect of military protocol in relation to UFO crash sites is the chain of command. Different branches of the military—Air Force, Army, Navy, and sometimes intelligence agencies—may become involved depending on the situation. Coordination can sometimes lead to confusion regarding responsibility and accountability, and the lack of a standardized approach has led to further speculation.

- **Intelligence Gathering**: Once the site is secured, intelligence units may step in to collect data. This involves taking photographs, securing samples, and retrieving any technology that can be feasibly transported.
- **Coordination with Higher Authorities**: Commanding officers will often work through the chain of command to gather interdisciplinary teams that may include scientists, technicians, and other specialists.
- **Declassification Levels**: Information gathered from such sites may be classified at various levels, leading to the selective release of information to the public, fueling further speculation.

Cover-Up or National Security?

One of the most contentious aspects of military responses to UFO crashes revolves around the perceived cover-up of information. Some skeptics see this as a blatant attempt to stifle public inquiry, while believers argue that national security rights do not give the government the privilege of withholding critical information about extraterrestrial life.

Key points often cited in discussions about military cover-ups include:

- **Misinformation**: Officials frequently issue contradictory statements regarding sightings and crash events. This can lead to confusion among the public and conspiracy theorists alike.
- **Limited Transparency**: Many investigations remain classified for decades, thus preventing historical analysis or scientific inquiry. The Roswell incident, for example, has evolved into a cultural phenomenon partly due to the lack of transparency from the military.
- **Witness Testimonies**: Military personnel often face challenges disclosing their experiences, fearing repercussions. This creates an environment ripe for conspiracy theories.

Historical Context: Notable Incidents

Looking back at historically notable incidents, we can discern patterns in military protocol and reactions:

- **Roswell (1947)**: Following the crash in New Mexico, military officials initially suggested that a "flying disc" had been recovered, only to retract that statement and label it a weather balloon. This confusing communication sparked decades of speculation and investigation.
- **Kecksburg Incident (1965)**: Witnesses reported seeing a fireball over Pennsylvania, leading to an immediate military intervention. Reports suggest that military personnel secured the site and removed what may have been extraterrestrial evidence.
- **Shag Harbour (1967)**: The Canadian military confirmed an

incident involving an unidentified submerged object. The military's cooperative stance in investigation contrasts sharply with the typical responses in the U.S., suggesting differing approaches to public engagement.

Conclusion

As we delve deeper into the historical framework surrounding UFO crash sites, we find that military protocols and reactions are complex and often contradictory. The interplay of secrecy, national security, and scientific curiosity establishes an intricate narrative that fuels ongoing speculation and investigation. In dissecting these incidents from a critical yet engaging perspective, we can better appreciate not only the clandestine world of military operations surrounding UFOs but also the enduring human fascination with the unknown.

9.3 Insights from Veterans

In the realm of UFO crash sites, the narratives woven by military veterans can provide invaluable insights, often blending firsthand accounts with the intricate tapestry of government secrecy, psychological ramifications, and the fight for acknowledgment of unexplained phenomena. Many veterans come forward with compelling stories that challenge official narratives and raise vital questions about what truly happened at these fabled locations.

Firsthand Accounts and Personal Motivations

Veterans recount their experiences from unique standpoints. Often, these individuals were involved in clean-up operations, investigations, or security details associated with alleged crash sites. Their stories, some decades old, can reveal much about the encounters with potential extraterrestrial debris and the subsequent aftermath. Important to note is the emotional and psychological weight these experiences carry.

- **Background in Military Operations**: Many of these veterans held significant roles during missions or operations that involved investigating unusual occurrences. Their familiarity with military protocol and procedures adds credibility to their accounts.
- **Personal Motivations**: A number of veterans come forward to reveal the truth behind the veil of secrecy, some seeking to clear their conscience while others aim for greater transparency regarding government interactions with UFOs.

Case Studies of Veterans' Testimonies

One of the most intriguing aspects of the UFO phenomenon is the reemergence of cases involving military veterans, each providing distinct perspectives related to alleged crash sites:

- **The Roswell Incident**: Perhaps the most famous UFO crash, the Roswell incident of 1947, has drawn numerous veterans to speak out. Many express a sense of duty to challenge the misinformation surrounding the event. Some maintain that the military was engaged in a disinformation campaign, claiming that what was retrieved from the site was far from conventional.
- **The Kecksburg Incident**: Veterans involved in the military response to the 1965 Kecksburg incident in Pennsylvania maintain that local reports of a UFO crash were quickly met with heavy military presence—seemingly to suppress information. Reports from the 1970s describe soldiers as witnesses looking at the downed object before being swiftly

ordered to keep quiet.

- **Area 51 and Other Bases**: Veterans who served at or near Area 51, a prominent hotbed for UFO speculation, recall unexplained activity that cannot be easily rationalized. They tell tales of increased UFO sightings and even interactions with unknown technology, raising questions about recovery operations associated with suspected extraterrestrial craft.

Common Themes Among Testimonies

Across various testimonies, certain themes emerge that characterize military veterans' accounts of UFO crash sites:

- **Secrecy and Cover-Ups**: Many veterans express frustration over the lack of transparency surrounding UFO incidents. Direct orders, they claim, were frequently issued to suppress disclosure.

- **Fear of Repercussions**: A recurring concern is the fear of career setbacks or personal stigma. This fear often led some veterans to remain silent for decades, with many only opening up after retirement.

- **Technical Descriptions**: Numerous veterans provide specific details that suggest advanced technology sparked their interest. Descriptions of unusual materials, propulsion mechanisms, or features lead to speculation about their origins and functions.

Psychological Impact

Beyond the tangible events, the psychological impact of these experiences cannot be understated. Many veterans report varying levels of anxiety, depression, or disillusionment:

- **Cognitive Dissonance**: Encountering something inexplicable juxtaposed against a lifetime of believing in conventional explanations creates mental tension. Veterans often grapple with reconciling what they witnessed with their training.

- **Stigma and Social Isolation**: Fear of ridicule and isolation is common, as many struggle to share their experiences with family and peers who may dismiss their claims.

Conclusion

The accounts of veterans associated with UFO crash sites form a crucial lens through which we examine this enigmatic phenomenon. Their stories not only highlight the potential for cover-ups that extend into the fabric of governmental operations but also emphasize the broader implications of what these events could mean for humanity's understanding of existence beyond our planet. As disclosure efforts ramp up and interest in UFOs grows, the voices of veterans will undoubtedly play a key role in shaping discourse and unraveling the historical narrative surrounding these mysterious incidents. Their insights remind us that the truth, elusive as it may be, continues to beckon for a more thorough exploration.

Chapter 10: The Allagash Abductions

10.1 A Gripping Tale of Unfolding Events

As the sun began to set on a warm July evening in 1947, the quiet expanse of the Roswell desert held secrets that would ripple through history for decades to come. The seemingly ordinary landscape became the stage for an extraordinary event that ignited speculation, conspiracy theories, and interest in the unknown—an event that would forever change the narrative surrounding UFOs in America. What followed was a gripping tale of unfolding events, deepening intrigue, and a quest for truth that remains unsolved.

The first indication that something unusual had occurred came from Mac Brazel, a rancher tending his livestock near Corona, New Mexico. On July 4, he discovered debris scattered across his property, which he initially thought might be linked to a downed weather balloon. As he sifted through the wreckage, something sparked his curiosity: it certainly was not conventional military equipment. A mishmash of metallic materials, strange symbols, and an unearthly sheen suggested a story far beyond the mundane explanations of the day.

Intrigued by the discovery, Brazel contacted the local authorities, who quickly alerted the military. The ensuing response would spiral into confusion and miscommunication. Truckloads of Army personnel descended upon the site, cordoning off the area and sealing it away from the public eye. Yet, rather than clearing the air, their actions only intensified speculation.

The next significant event came when the Roswell Army Air Field issued a press release declaring that they had recovered a "flying disc." The announcement sent shockwaves through the community, capturing sensational headlines across the nation. However, the euphoria of this revelation was short-lived. Just a day later, the military retracted its statement, claiming it was nothing more than a weather balloon, an explanation many deemed inadequate.

This swift reversal in the official narrative left the public mystified and primed for speculation. Questions emerged about the authenticity of the wreckage and the nature of the materials. What did the military know that they weren't willing to share? Why the cover-up? These queries spurred a plethora of theories about not only the Roswell incident but the existence of extraterrestrial life itself.

As tales of the crash spread, the atmosphere became rife with speculation and investigative fervor. Some insisted that the wreckage was part of a top-secret military project. Others started whispering about the vehicle's occupants—claims of recovered bodies, their features enigmatic and unlike anything humans had ever seen. These rumors were seemingly supported by a handful of witnesses who claimed they had seen military vehicles transporting more than just metal scraps into the dark recesses of a nearby facility.

Various accounts began to emerge:

- Witnesses describing strange lights in the night sky on the night of the crash
- Military personnel reportedly silencing those who dared to speak openly about the event
- Futuristic materials that defied understanding and sparked imaginations

UFO CRASH SITES

The intrigue intensified when the first manuscripts and testimonies began to surface, chronicling personal experiences of alleged UFO sightings in conjunction with the Roswell incident. A myriad of stories bloomed through the passionate voice of local residents, some claiming that strange objects were seen in the sky near ranches, while others spoke of odd occurrences in the days following the crash.

What added a layer of complexity to the narrative was a network of supposed government professionals who had purportedly been involved in retrieving and studying the wreckage. Their drafty, hesitant interviews hinted at a deeper conspiracy at play, revealing a belief that not only had a craft landed—or crashed—but that the recovery effort was potentially part of a larger hidden agenda.

As the years continued to roll on, the Roswell incident laid the groundwork for burgeoning UFO lore that would permeate into the global consciousness. Conferences began popping up, investigative documentaries gained traction, and the term "flying saucer" entered mainstream lexicon. People from all walks of life became involved—enthusiasts, scientists, skeptics—each contributing to the whirlpool of interest surrounding extraterrestrial phenomena.

Through painstaking investigation, clandestine testimonies, and cultural curiosity, the Roswell crash remains a pivotal event in the annals of UFO history. The initial tantalizing tales of metal, Morris Code devices, and otherworldly beings have morphed into an urgent pursuit of understanding—one that transcends the boundaries of rationality and beckons humanity to consider the larger cosmos. As new evidence emerges and old records are examined, the story of what really happened on that fateful July day continues to unfold, promising revelations that have yet to be fully grasped.

10.2 Hypnosis and Memories

The practice of hypnosis has often found itself entwined with reports of UFO encounters and crashes, especially when it comes to eliciting memories from individuals who claim to have experienced such events firsthand. This intersection raises intriguing questions about the nature of memory, the reliability of eyewitness accounts, and the psychological mechanisms at play in alleged abduction or crash site witnesses.

The Role of Hypnosis

Hypnosis is a technique that can facilitate a trance-like state, allowing individuals to access deeper layers of consciousness. This tool has been implemented by investigators to help subjects recall details they might otherwise forget or suppress. Proponents argue that hypnosis can uncover hidden memories associated with UFO sightings or encounters, unlocking information that could provide significant insights into these elusive phenomena.

However, the relationship between hypnosis and memory is complex. While this technique can sometimes lead to the recall of genuine experiences, it can also produce false memories or distort existing ones. This duality warrants a closer examination.

The Mechanisms of Memory

Human memory is inherently malleable. Psychologists emphasize the following points regarding how memories form, change, and sometimes deceive:

- **Constructive Nature of Memory**: Memories are not perfect records of past events; they are reconstructed each time we recall them. This means that external influences and suggestions can alter them.

- **Suggestibility**: Individuals under hypnosis are often more suggestible, making them susceptible to incorporating inaccurate details suggested by the hypnotist or other external sources into their recollections.

- **Confabulation**: This is a natural process where the brain fills in gaps in memory with fabricated details, which the individual believes to be true.

Case Studies

Numerous cases have highlighted the use of hypnosis among UFO witnesses, leading to both startling revelations and significant skepticism:

- **The Betty and Barney Hill Case (1961)**: This dotted the landscape of UFO abduction narratives. Under hypnosis, both Betty and Barney recounted detailed accounts of their supposed abduction, including descriptions of the extraterrestrial beings involved. However, later scrutiny revealed inconsistencies and prompted debates on the reliability of the memories retrieved.

- **The Allagash Waterway Incident (1976)**: Four men reported seeing a bright light while camping and later underwent hypnosis to recover additional details. Their sessions led to vivid accounts of an encounter with a UFO and alien beings. Critics pointed to the synchronicity of their recollections, suggesting the memories may have been influenced by the communal nature of their hypnosis sessions.

Ethical Considerations

The use of hypnosis in researching UFO experiences raises ethical questions, particularly regarding informed consent and the responsibility of the investigator. When manipulating memory, it is essential to maintain a careful balance between seeking the truth and potentially causing harm to the witnesses' psychological well-being. Hypnosis should never be viewed as a definitive tool but rather as one method among many in investigating these extraordinary claims.

The Scientific Community's Perspective

While some researchers accept hypnosis as a valid method for recovering trauma-related memories, skepticism remains prevalent. Here are the primary viewpoints within the scientific community:

- **Skeptical View**: Critics argue that the artificiality of retrieved memories could lead to false recall, significantly clouding the credibility of reported experiences.

- **Supportive View**: Some psychologists advocate for the careful, controlled use of hypnosis, believing it provides richer data when corroborated with other forms of evidence.

Concluding Thoughts

The intersection of hypnosis and memories related to UFO crash sites is a nuanced and controversial area of study. While hypnosis remains a compelling tool for attempting to peel back the layers of human memory, it is fraught with the potential for error and manipulation. For enthusiasts and researchers alike, it acts as both an avenue for uncovering truths and a cautionary tale about the delicate nature of memory itself.

As the debate continues about the reliability of hypnotically retrieved memories, the importance of integrating diverse methodologies—such as witness interviews, corroborating physical evidence, and historical context—cannot be overstated in the pursuit of understanding UFO phenomena and their associated mysteries. The quest for clarity stands at the frontier of what may or may not be hidden in the depths of our collective consciousness.

10.3 Skepticism and Support

In the exploration of UFO crash sites, a crucial aspect to consider is the duality of skepticism and support that permeates the conversation. The phenomenon of UFOs, far from being purely the domain of enthusiasts and believers, invites a multitude of perspectives, from staunch proponents of extraterrestrial involvement to rigorous skeptics who demand empirical evidence. This interplay significantly shapes the narrative surrounding purported crash sites, influencing public perception and scientific inquiry.

The Skeptics' Perspective

Skeptics often approach claims of UFO crash sites with a healthy dose of skepticism, prioritizing critical thinking and an empirical method of investigation. Many argue that extraordinary claims require extraordinary evidence, and they are determined to scrutinize the reports surrounding such incidents. Key points they raise include:

- **Lack of Reliable Evidence**: Skeptics often question the authenticity of the evidence presented, emphasizing the absence of physical artifacts or credible eyewitness accounts that withstand scrutiny over time. They argue that many claims rely too heavily on anecdotal evidence or sensationalized media reports.

- **Alternative Explanations**: Many skeptics propose alternative explanations for UFO sightings or crashes, attributing them to natural phenomena, misidentified aircraft, or psychological factors like mass hallucinations. For instance, meteorological balloons or secret military tests could easily account for unidentified flying objects or supposed wreckage.

- **Historial Context and Hoaxes**: Historical context can often illuminate why certain crash sites gained notoriety. The Roswell incident is frequently cited, with skeptics highlighting how social and political climates gave rise to hoaxes and conspiracy theories. The popular culture of the time framed this narrative, leading to a proliferation of claims that may be rooted in misunderstandings.

The Supporters' Argument

In stark contrast, supporters of the UFO crash hypothesis argue for the validity of these events, often citing various incidents where they believe credible evidence aligns with the presence of extraterrestrial technology. Their key arguments often include:

- **Eyewitness Accounts**: Proponents emphasize the weight of testimony from military personnel, locals, or credible figures. When these testimonies come from those with technical expertise, they argue that it adds legitimacy to the claims of UFO crashes.

- **Physical Evidence**: While skeptics claim a lack of reliable evidence, supporters highlight instances where unusual materials, alleged metal samples, or unexplained technologies have been retrieved and analyzed, even if findings have often been inconclusive. They contend that experimentation and transparency in analysis have yet to be fully realized.

- **Government Secrecy**: Supporters argue that government denial or silence often bolsters the belief in cover-ups related to UFO crash sites. This theory posits that agencies like the U.S. Air Force or CIA have intentionally withheld information to mask interactions with extraterrestrial technology, especially during high-profile incidents like Roswell or the Phoenix Lights.

Case Studies: A Balanced Lens

The primary noted incidents provide valuable insight into both sides of the argument. The Roswell incident of 1947 remains the most famous UFO crash site, characterized by a long-standing debate between believers and skeptics. Reports of a "flying disk" quickly shifted to military claims of a weather balloon, fuelling speculation regarding how information was managed and disseminated.

- **Roswell, New Mexico**: Major witness testimony, alongside military cover-up narratives, has kept this case alive in the annals of UFO history.

- **Kecksburg, Pennsylvania**: The incident in 1965 saw a fireball across the sky and subsequent military recovery efforts. Both skeptics and believers found fuel for their arguments in contradictory narratives.

- **Shag Harbour, Nova Scotia**: In 1967, witnesses claimed to see an object crash into the waters. The Royal Canadian Mounted Police (RCMP) reported official documentation, sparking debates on governmental distinction and involvement.

The Middle Ground

Navigating the landscape between skepticism and support is vital for advanced discussions surrounding UFO crash sites. Both sides offer important insights and contribute to a broader understanding of the phenomena. Intellectual humility can lead to fruitful exploration of these incidents:

- **Encouraging Open Dialogue**: The intersection of skepticism and belief encourages ongoing conversation, inviting researchers from varied backgrounds—scientific, historical, and cultural—to investigate the mysteries of UFO sightings collaboratively.

- **Scientific Inquiry**: Salvation for the UFO community may lie in a unified, methodical scientific approach that seeks to document, analyze, and investigate these claims without bias.

In summary, the dynamic between skepticism and support regarding UFO crash sites serves as a potent reminder of the complexity of truth-seeking in the realms of the extraordinary. Each viewpoint contributes vital context to what continues to be a captivating, albeit contentious, debate. Whether believers or skeptics, the quest for understanding remains a compelling part of our exploration of the unknown.

Chapter 11: The Rendlesham Forest Case

11.1 A Night of Strange Lights

As the sun dipped below the horizon on April 24, 1980, residents of the small town of Cash-Landrum, Texas, wouldn't have expected that their night would be marked by one of the most compelling UFO incidents in history. It began with a peculiar glow in the sky, one that shifted and danced beyond the realm of standard aircraft. For Betty Cash, Vickie Landrum, and Colby Landrum, the event that unfolded would change their lives forever, prompting questions about not only what they had witnessed but also what lay hidden within the anomalous lights.

An Enigmatic Encounter

The Cash-Landrum incident is notable not only for the peculiar lights described by the witnesses but also for the surrounding circumstances that accompanied the experience. As Betty, Vickie, and Colby were driving home from a bingo game, they suddenly noticed bright, fiery objects in the sky. These unusual shapes emitted an intense light that flickered between various colors, giving off a sense of urgency and mystery.

Betty described the lights as resembling a large diamond shape, hovering silently at a low altitude. Vickie, who was in the car alongside her, recalled the overwhelming intensity of the lights that seemed to pulse with energy. Despite being filled with trepidation, the three felt compelled to stop the car and observe the phenomenon. They pulled over to the side of the road, their eyes glued to the sky, captivated yet fearful of what could be unfolding above them.

A Rising Intensity

As they stared up at the luminous spectacle, they noticed the lights shifting positions, almost as if they were communicating through dance. The three witnesses watched in tense silence, eventually noting a sudden change: the fiery objects began to descend, hovering closer to the ground. This was not merely strange; it was chilling. The lights had now transformed into a more identifiable shape—an apparent craft.

- **Witness Descriptions:**

Betty Cash: Noted the bright lights appearing diamond-shaped, spinning in a slow motion.

Vickie Landrum: Suggested the lights communicated with each other, intensifying and dimming in a rhythmic pattern.

Colby Landrum: Captured the event through the eyes of a young boy, feeling both awe and fear for the unknown presence above.

At that moment, everything changed. A loud blast of heat surged toward them, followed by a strange, metallic-sounding roar. The very air around them felt electrified, causing their hearts to race. Even days after, Betty would describe feeling a compelling, almost magnetic pull toward the dazzling craft.

The Aftermath

What transpired after the event was just as perplexing as the sighting itself. Over the following days and weeks, the witnesses began to experience a myriad of health issues. The trio suffered from severe ailments including:

- **Skin burns**: Betty Cash reported blisters resembling burns on her skin, which perplexed her physician.

- **Respiratory problems**: Vickie Landrum experienced unsettling respiratory complications, leading to chronic coughing.
- **Psychological impact**: Colby displayed fear and anxiety, troubled by nightmares centered around the incident.

In their search for understanding, Betty Cash and her allies sought medical attention and various explanations from officials. They reached out to local authorities, only to be met with skepticism. This lack of support prompted further investigation into their claims, attracting the attention of ufologists and even making its way into local news.

The Broader Context: Societal Implications

The Cash-Landrum case serves as a critical touchpoint in understanding how encounters with unexplained phenomena can ripple through the fabric of society. It raises several vital questions:

- **How are witnesses treated post-encounter?** Skepticism often leads to isolation for those who report sightings.
- **What are the psychological impacts?** The lingering effects can be profound, leading to chronic health issues.
- **Could there be an underlying government cover-up?** The questions surrounding potential military involvement add layers to the mystery, further fueling conspiracy theories that have persisted well into modern times.

Conclusion

Ultimately, the night of strange lights in Cash-Landrum became more than just a fleeting moment of wonder and fear; it evolved into an enduring story of intrigue, suspicion, and unanswered questions. As the search for truth continued, those who witnessed the event became unwitting ambassadors for a broader dialogue about UFOs and the mysteries they often bring with them. This peculiar encounter serves as a reminder that, even in the darkest nights when strange lights dance across the sky, the quest for knowledge remains ever luminous.

11.2 Military Investigations

The investigation of UFO crash sites has always piqued the interest of researchers, history buffs, and conspiracy theorists alike. Among the most compelling facets of these investigations is the heavy involvement of military organizations, which often communicate an air of confidentiality and urgency that only adds to the intrigue surrounding these encounters. This section delves into various military investigations of UFO crash sites, shining a light on how national defense has intersected with unidentified aerial phenomena.

Historical Context

The United States military's interest in UFOs can be traced back to World War II when pilots reported encountering unidentified flying objects during air combat. These encounters led to a growing concern that enemy forces could possess advanced aerial technology. This budding interest rapidly escalated after the infamous Roswell incident in July 1947, where an object reportedly crashed on a ranch in New Mexico. Initially described as a "flying disc," the military quickly retracted this statement, claiming it was merely a weather balloon—a narrative that would become a cornerstone in UFO lore.

Notable Military Investigations

Throughout the decades, several significant military investigations into UFO crash sites have taken place, each with its unique set of complexities and implications:

- **Project Blue Book (1952-1969)**: This U.S. Air Force program was launched to assess UFO sightings and analyze potential threats. Project Blue Book investigated numerous crash sites, gathering data and attempting to debunk as many sightings as possible. While officially disbanded in 1969, it laid the groundwork for understanding the military's handling of UFO phenomena.

- **The Roswell Incident (1947)**: Perhaps the most famous of all alleged UFO crash incidents, the Roswell event has been the subject of extensive investigation and speculation. The military's initial report of a "flying disc" was quickly revised to a "weather balloon," leading many to speculate about a government cover-up. The incident remains a focal point for those supporting the existence of extraterrestrial life and government concealment.

- **The Kecksburg Incident (1965)**: This lesser-known case occurred in Pennsylvania, where residents reported seeing a fireball in the sky followed by a crash. The military responded promptly, cordoning off the area and recovering debris, which was later alleged to have been an extraterrestrial craft. The details surrounding this incident remain murky, fueling conspiracy theories.

- **The Rendlesham Forest Incident (1980)**: Often referred to as "Britain's Roswell," this series of reported UFO sightings near a military base in Suffolk, England involved U.S. Air Force personnel who witnessed strange lights and unexplained phenomena. Official accounts suggest extensive military investigations were conducted, but the findings remained classified, prompting speculation on what the military actually discovered.

Military Protocols and Response

Responses to UFO crash site investigations often involve strict protocols, including:

- **Immediate Isolation**: Military personnel typically secure the area surrounding a reported crash site to prevent civilian interference and potential exposure of sensitive information.

- **Damage Assessment**: Teams assess the crash site for potential dangers, including hazardous materials or unexploded ordnance.

- **Debris Recovery**: The military often collects fragments and other remnants, which are then analyzed in controlled environments.

- **Intelligence Gathering**: Beyond physical evidence, military investigations typically aim to gather intelligence on witness accounts, monitoring for anomalous activities.

Influence on Public Perception

The military's involvement in UFO investigations has significantly shaped cultural perceptions. Their apparent secrecy and lack of transparency have led many to believe that a deeper truth regarding extraterrestrial life exists, further stoking public curiosity and conspiracy theories. The dichotomy between official statements and public speculation fosters a sense of mistrust, prompting ongoing debates on governmental accountability.

Conclusion

Military investigations into UFO crash sites remain one of the most captivating enigmas within the broader narrative of unidentified flying objects. The intersection of fact and speculation offers a fertile ground for researchers and enthusiasts, fostering both scholarly discourse and popular intrigue. As technology evolves and more information becomes accessible, the layers of these investigations will hopefully peel back, revealing the true nature behind these fascinating phenomena.

In exploring military investigations, we uncover not only the methods employed in assessing these intriguing events but also the impact on contemporary understanding of UFOs. With each newfound piece of evidence or account, the narrative grows richer, encouraging a continued pursuit of knowledge in this uncharted territory of history and the paranormal.

11.3 Impact on UK-US Relations

The enigma of UFO crash sites has not only captured the public's imagination but has also had significant implications for international relations, particularly between the United Kingdom and the United States. The enduring interest and speculation surrounding these incidents offer a unique insight into the nature of cooperation, secrecy, and distrust between these two nations during the latter half of the 20th century.

Historical Context

During the Cold War, when geopolitical tensions were high, both the UK and the US were actively engaged in intelligence-gathering and national security efforts. The possibility of UFO sightings often coincided with heightened military activity—leading to questions about whether these phenomena were extraterrestrial or merely advanced technology from rival nations.

The notorious Roswell incident of 1947, while occurring in the United States, piqued British interest as rumors of a secret military research program began to surface. By the 1950s, reports of flying saucers emerged globally, and UFO phenomena became an essential topic in governmental discussions about defense and security strategies. It was in this environment that the UK and the US began to tread carefully in sharing information about their findings on UFOs.

Collaboration and Secrecy

The impact of UFO investigations on UK-US relations can be categorized into two major areas: collaboration and secrecy.

Collaboration

1. **Joint Military Exercises**: During the Cold War, both nations engaged in joint military exercises, where aerial phenomena were often scrutinized. These exercises produced reports that sometimes included references to unidentified aerial phenomena.

2. **Information Sharing**: As the interest in UFOs surged, there were instances where classified information was shared between British and American intelligence agencies. A notable example is the exchange over the investigation of the 1952 Washington, D.C. UFO sightings, which prompted considerable discussion on both sides of the Atlantic.

3. **Cultural Exchange**: The fascination with UFOs incentivized cultural exchanges that encouraged citizens from both nations to explore and document local sightings. This grassroots level of investigation helped build a mutual interest in the phenomenon, creating a shared narrative that went beyond official reports.

Secrecy

1. **Top-Secret Programs**: The classification of UFO-related reports under national security protocols meant that much information remained in the shadows. Programs such as Project Blue Book in the US were married to the secrecy surrounding similar investigations in the UK, including the Ministry of Defence's Project Condign, which led to suspicions regarding the extent of knowledge either nation held.

2. **Conspiracy Theories**: As the public clamored for transparency concerning UFOs, the lack of available information fostered conspiracy theories that thrived on the idea of government cover-ups. This environment of distrust often strained how citizens perceived their gov-

ernments and each other. Individuals in both nations began to question what was being kept from them, leading to calls for investigations from outside researchers and advocates.

3. **Diplomatic Tensions**: Reports of close encounters or sightings near military installations, especially during periods of heightened tension (like the Cuban Missile Crisis), strained diplomatic relations. Mutual distrust over potential accidental confrontations contributed to an air of secrecy designed to protect national security interests.

Public Response and Influence

The growing public interest in UFOs has acted as a barometer for shifting perceptions about both governments' transparency. The release of various classified documents over the decades has often sparked renewed discussions about the nature of these phenomena and their implications for international relations.

1. **Media Coverage**: The sensationalization of UFO reports in the press has often led to public outrage concerning government transparency. In the UK, coverage of UFO sightings and subsequent denials from the government created a rift between public perception and official rhetoric.

2. **Advocacy Groups**: Organizations such as the British UFO Research Association and American UFO groups have pushed both governments to assist in the matter of unexplained aerial phenomena, advocating for a more open dialogue around military encounters and investigations.

3. **Legislative Action**: The recent movements within the US Congress to investigate UFOs have had ripple effects in the UK, prompting similar calls for transparency and generating renewed interest in shared intelligence regarding unidentified aerial phenomena.

Conclusion

In summary, the impact of UFO crash sites on UK-US relations is multifaceted, rife with collaboration borne of security needs and secrecy stemming from national interest. The continued exploration of these phenomena serves as a fascinating backdrop to understanding how both nations interact in an ever-complex global framework. As more information becomes available and public pressure mounts for transparency, it stands to reason that the intricacies of these historical interactions will persistently influence diplomatic relations between the UK and the US.

Chapter 12: The Phoenix Lights Revisited

12.1 Witness Testimonies

Witness testimonies regarding UFO crash sites offer a vital channel into understanding the events that surround these enigmatic occurrences. While conspiracy theories and government cover-ups often dominate the dialogues surrounding UFOs, the firsthand accounts from individuals who claim to have witnessed these incidents provide a different, more human perspective on what may have transpired.

Over the decades, numerous reports have emerged from various regions across the globe, detailing unexpected encounters with unidentified flying objects. These accounts range from military personnel to everyday citizens, revealing a spectrum of experiences that demand rigorous exploration.

Significant Cases

Several key incidents have solidified themselves within the UFO lore, drawing myriad eyewitnesses into their narratives. Below are some of the most notable cases linked to alleged UFO crashes:

- **Roswell Incident (1947)**: Perhaps the most infamous case, reports from locals in New Mexico describe seeing wreckage and military personnel securing the site. Eyewitnesses claimed metallic debris, mysterious symbols, and even, allegedly, extraterrestrial bodies.

- **Kecksburg Incident (1965)**: Witness testimonies from Pennsylvania recount a fireball streaking across the sky, followed by the discovery of a bronze acorn-shaped object. Individuals observed military vehicles arriving and restricting access to the area where the object landed.

- **Val Johnson Case (1979)**: Deputy Sheriff Val Johnson's encounter in Minnesota has intrigued UFO enthusiasts for years. Johnson reported a close encounter with a bright light that resulted in damage to his patrol car, which many view as indirect evidence of a potential UFO crash.

The witnesses in these instances have provided crucial details, whether corroborating UFO features or the sudden military presence, which stoked public curiosity and conspiracy theories alike.

Common Themes in Testimonies

A close analysis of various testimonies reveals recurring themes that appear in many accounts. Some points of significance include:

- **Unusual Craft Characteristics**: Witnesses describe the crafts as often having metallic surfaces, unique forms (saucer-shaped, acorn-shaped), and lighting systems that defy conventional aerodynamic design.

- **Government Intervention**: Many testimonies report immediate military presence post-incident, with personnel allegedly working to secure and clean the crash sites. Eyewitnesses often mention unusual control mechanisms, such as barricades and sudden evacuation orders.

- **Mysterious Bodies**: A handful of accounts, particularly within the Roswell reports, include claims of seeing humanoid figures, with descriptions ranging from small and alien-like to more ambiguous humanoid shapes.

- **Time Anomalies**: Witnesses frequently report time discrepancies, claiming they lost hours while at the scene or later recalling events differently than they envisioned moments before.

The Impact of Eyewitness Accounts

Eyewitness testimonies play an essential role in both shaping public perception and advancing research in the field of UFO investigations. Their importance can be summarized as follows:

- **Humanizing the Phenomenon**: Personal accounts transform UFO incidents from abstract theories into relatable experiences, making it easier for people to engage with the subject matter.

- **Data Collection**: As researchers gather testimonies, they create databases that can reveal trends and recurring patterns, offering potential leads to where further investigation is warranted.

- **Sparking Interest**: The recounting of alien encounters or close encounters can reignite interest in UFO phenomena, driving grassroots movements for disclosure and further research.

Skepticism and Credibility

While witness testimonies can provide valuable insights, it's important to approach them cautiously, bearing in mind the vast potential for misinterpretation or sensationalism. Various factors can influence the reliability of these accounts, such as:

- **Psychological Factors**: The human mind can play tricks — vivid dreams, sensory overload, or even hallucinations can contribute to altered perceptions of reality.

- **Social Influence**: Pre-existing beliefs or cultural narratives about UFOs can shape how witnesses interpret their experiences, leading to biases.

- **Misinformation**: Some accounts may emerge from a context of fear or panic, particularly in sensationalized news portrayals or local folklore.

In considering the rich tapestry of testimonies surrounding UFO crash sites, it is critical to balance the personal insights offered by witnesses with an analytical perspective rooted in skepticism. As UFO investigation continues to evolve, the stories shared by witnesses remain one of the most compelling aspects of understanding these perplexing phenomena. Through their accounts, the mystery transforms into an intriguing narrative that demands further investigation and discourse among enthusiasts, researchers, and the inspired populace.

12.2 Scientific Analysis

The examination of UFO crash sites through scientific analysis not only invigorates the quest for understanding potential extraterrestrial encounters but also solidifies or refutes anecdotal claims with empirical data. As researchers sift through the wreckage of alleged extraterrestrial crafts, they employ a variety of scientific methods to ascertain the authenticity and implications of these incidents.

One major landmark case that opened the floodgates for scientific inquiry was the Roswell Incident of 1947. Initially debunked as a "weather balloon" recovery, subsequent analyses brought renewed interest and skepticism, inviting researchers from multiple fields to engage in a thorough investigation of the purported crash site and its implications. This has served as a template for scientific analysis that can be applied to other reported sites.

Techniques Used in Scientific Analysis
1. Geophysical Surveys

Geophysical techniques, such as Magnetic Resonance Imaging (MRI) and Ground Penetrating Radar (GPR), have become staples in the analysis of crash sites. These non-invasive methods allow researchers to detect subsurface anomalies without disturbing the ground. Common findings include:

- **Irregularities in soil composition** that may indicate an object's presence.
- **Metallic signatures**, which can suggest foreign materials, potentially from craft.
- **Disturbed earth patterns**, hinting at excavation or impact zones.

2. Sample Collection and Analysis

To validate claims of extraterrestrial material, scientists collect samples from the site. These are subsequently analyzed using:

- **Spectroscopy** to identify elemental and molecular composition.
- **Isotope analysis** which can reveal unusual signatures not typically found on Earth.
- **Microscopic examinations** to look for anomalies at the

microscopic level, including possible contamination sources.

3. Witness Testimonies and Historical Context

While not a conventional scientific analysis method, the context in which a UFO crash occurs is vital. Researchers often evaluate:

- **Eyewitness accounts** for consistency and reliability.
- **Historical documents** that provide background on military activities or weather phenomena that could explain or debunk the incident.
- **Cultural narratives** surrounding the events—sometimes crucial for understanding local beliefs and responses.

Interdisciplinary Collaboration

The investigation of UFO crash sites often requires the collaboration of multiple disciplines. Archaeologists, physicists, and materials scientists participate in these studies, each contributing unique skills and perspectives. This multidisciplinary approach yields richer insights and promotes a more nuanced understanding of findings.

Case Studies of Scientific Investigation

The Roswell Incident (1947)

Following the famous recovery of debris, several studies have focused on soil samples from the alleged crash site. In 2005, researchers collected soil from various areas, detecting isotopic anomalies that suggested the presence of various elements unknown to conventional Earth materials. These analyses have led to fervent debates about the material's origin and composition.

The Kecksburg Incident (1965)

Another notable case involves the Kecksburg UFO incident, where locals claimed to have witnessed a fiery object crash in Pennsylvania. Scientific investigations into the area included aerial surveys and ground analysis. Remarkably, some researchers posited that the site contained traces of a non-terrestrial material—resulting in a flurry of scientific interest and media attention.

Challenges in Scientific Analysis

Despite advancements, scientists face formidable challenges when examining UFO crash sites:

- **High Degree of Secrecy**: Governmental restrictions often inhibit access to sites, leading to speculation about cover-ups.
- **Material Degradation**: Depending on the crash timeline, materials may have degraded or been removed entirely, complicating analyses.
- **Bias and Preconceptions**: Scientific inquiry must contend with inherent biases that may cloud objective investigation, given the sensational nature of UFO lore.

The Role of Technology

Emerging technologies such as drones equipped with advanced imaging capabilities, alongside artificial intelligence algorithms for pattern recognition, are enhancing our ability to sift through substantial datasets. These innovations promise to transform UFO crash site investigations, offering unprecedented detail and analysis of phenomena typically relegated to the realm of pseudoscience.

Conclusion

The scientific analysis of UFO crash sites exemplifies the interplay between inquiry and skepticism in understanding potential alien encounters. By prioritizing empirical methodologies and interdisciplinary efforts, researchers attempt to uncover the truth behind enigmatic events, oscillating between the lines of history, science, and the extraordinary. As technology continues to evolve, so too does our capacity to parse the smudgy boundaries between fact and fiction in the UFO narrative.

12.3 Cultural Repercussions

Across the vast tapestry of human culture, few subjects inspire the collective imagination quite like the phenomenon of UFO crash sites. These locations, often shrouded in mystery and speculation, not only provoke intense interest among UFO enthusiasts but also serve as cultural touchstones that reflect societal fears, aspirations, and curiosities. Historical incidents, such as the alleged Roswell crash in 1947, have left indelible marks upon popular culture, influencing the way in which extraterrestrial encounters are perceived and discussed.

Fragmented Narratives and National Identity

The cultural repercussions of UFO crash sites often extend into the realms of national identity and collective memory. In the aftermath of high-profile incidents, narratives surrounding these events frequently become fragmented, encompassing myth, rumor, and politicized interpretations. For many, the mythos surrounding a crash site can serve as a means to question governmental transparency and accountability.

- **Governments and Secrecy**: The storied government cover-ups associated with UFO incidents, particularly in the United States, have resulted in a pervasive belief that authorities withhold crucial information from the public.
- **Distrust in Institutions**: This growing skepticism often amplifies proposals of conspiracy theories, enriching folklore surrounding crash sites. As a result, communities may develop a mistrust that transcends individual incidents, fostering a culture of inquiry about the very nature of reality.

Influences on Creative Media

Beyond the realm of conspiracy and institutional critique, UFO crash sites have significantly influenced creative media. The stories of alien encounters, government conspiracies, and crash recoveries enter the realm of imagination, driving the creation of movies, literature, and television shows that explore these themes in engaging ways.

- **Film and Television**: Iconic films such as "Close Encounters of the Third Kind" and series like "The X-Files" have rooted themselves in the lore of these events, capturing the fascination of audiences eager to understand the unknown.
- **Literature and Comics**: From novels to graphic novels, the narratives revolving around UFO crashes can trigger deep philosophical questions about humanity's place in the cosmos.

The trope of the UFO crash not only entertains but often invites a deeper exploration of humanity's existential dilemmas, thus creating an exchange between artistic expression and cultural inquiry.

Shaping Subcultures

The lore of UFO crash sites has led to the emergence of subcultures centered around belief systems that embrace the notion of extraterrestrial life. Meetings, associations, and gatherings of UFO enthusiasts perpetuate belief in these narratives, allowing followers to connect, share experiences, and disseminate information.

- **Conventions and Expositions**: Events such as UFO festivals celebrate the cultural significance of crash sites, often featuring speakers, researchers, and enthusiasts who discuss their findings.
- **Online Communities**: Websites and forums dedicated to UFO discussions provide platforms for sharing theories,

research, and personal anecdotes concerning alleged crashes and sightings.

These subcultures serve as vital networks for those seeking validation of their beliefs, connecting individuals through shared experiences and histories that may otherwise remain hidden.

Influence on Science and Technology

Curiously, the fascination with UFO crash sites has also sparked interest in scientific inquiry and technological advancement. The notion of reverse engineering alien technology, as purportedly pursued after incidents like Roswell, has caught the attention of inventors, scientists, and futurists.

- **Innovative Research**: The search for extraterrestrial life leads to significant advancements in fields such as space exploration, physics, and engineering.
- **Public Interest in Science**: The intersection of UFOs and science creates public enthusiasm for STEM (Science, Technology, Engineering, and Mathematics) fields, as younger generations are inspired to question and explore the universe.

Conclusion

The cultural repercussions stemming from UFO crash sites span a wide array of influences, from reshaping national narratives to inspiring creative expressions and scientific inquiry. These sites serve as focal points of obsession, inquiry, and creativity, challenging the boundaries of belief while inviting vehement debates. While the veracity of the events surrounding UFO crashes may remain contentious, their impact on culture, identity, and community is indisputable. These intersecting realms of existence paint a complex picture, where history, folklore, and science converge to form a rich narrative tapestry that continues to evolve. In essence, UFO crash sites do more than just represent points of impact; they symbolize our deep-seated quest for knowledge in an unfathomable universe.

Chapter 13: The Shag Harbour Incident

13.1 Discovery of the Unidentified Object

The phenomenon of unidentified flying objects (UFOs) has intrigued humanity for decades, opening doors to various theories that often blur the lines between fact and fiction. Within this enigmatic realm lies a disturbing and compelling subject: UFO crash sites. One of the most notable incidents that fueled the world's fascination occurred in July 1947 in Roswell, New Mexico, where the discovery of an unidentified object would alter the landscape of both UFO lore and government secrecy.

On July 8, 1947, local rancher Mac Brazel stumbled upon a mysterious wreckage in the New Mexico desert, approximately 75 miles from Roswell. What he initially presumed to be a downed weather balloon quickly drew his attention due to its unusual materials. According to Brazel's accounts and later interviews, the debris did not resemble anything he had encountered before; it was described as a mix of metallic parts, rubber-like substances, and strange, hieroglyphic-like symbols embossed on the materials.

Brazel was hesitant to report his discovery, fearing it might be an illegal crash from military operations. However, after discussions with nearby neighbors and subsequent news coverage, he brought the matter to the attention of the local authorities. The Roswell Army Air Field

(RAAF) was alerted, effectively kicking off a series of events that would lead to an enormous cover-up and set the stage for one of the most notorious UFO incidents in history.

Initial Investigations

When military personnel arrived to investigate the site, they initially appeared intrigued and somewhat astonished by the findings. According to reports, they collected the debris and brought it back to the base. However, the narrative quickly shifted when a press release from the military indicated that the discovered debris had been nothing more than a fallen "weather balloon." This was met with skepticism by many, including researchers and conspiracy theorists, who predominately felt that the government was trying to mask the reality of what had been found.

Features of the Discovery

As details emerged, a few features of the unidentified object gained considerable attention:

- **Unusual Material Composition:** Witnesses described materials that were incredibly light yet impossible to destroy. For instance, witnesses noted that when they attempted to crumple the metallic subsamples, they would instantly return to their original shape.

- **Potential Origin:** Some individuals and researchers speculated that the object might not be of this Earth. This perspective set off a torrent of speculation regarding extraterrestrial technology and its implications, forever intertwining UFO lore with ideas of alien visitations.

- **Witness Testimonies:** Numerous witnesses came forward in the weeks and months that followed, claiming they had seen strange lights in the sky on the dates surrounding the crash.

These testimonials only increased intrigue and suspicion surrounding the government's version of events.

The Fallout from the Discovery

The aftermath of the Roswell incident sparked an obsession with crash sites among UFO enthusiasts, historians, and for many – conspiracy theorists. It broadened the search for other suspected extraterrestrial events across the globe. Not long after Roswell, similar events began to emerge in reports from various rural and isolated locations. Each suggested the possibility of further unidentified crafts that either crashed or landed, leading to various government investigations.

The consequences of the Roswell incident blurred the lines between investigation and hysteria. Skepticism towards the government assertions became rampant, encapsulated by the following thoughts:

- **Cover-up Theories:** Many theorists argue that the military operated under an extensive cover-up, perpetuating a narrative to maintain control over classified information and hush the public's curiosity.

- **Cultural Impact:** The Roswell incident ignited an explosion in UFO-themed literature, media, and festivals in subsequent decades. It has been referenced in movies, documentaries, and even homegrown conceits that idealized or vilified aliens.

Conclusion

Though officially dismissed as a weather balloon, the Roswell event established the archetype for UFO crash site theories, serving as a foundation for ensuing investigations into other sightings and suspected crash locations worldwide. It raised essential questions about our understanding of extraterrestrial life and the extent of government loyalty to the broader population.

Are we witnessing the remnants of advanced technology beyond our comprehension, or are these merely figments of an imaginative society? The inquiry continues unabated, propelling UFO enthusiasts and researchers alike into a quest for truth in the shadowy world of unidentified flying objects, their crash sites, and what they might reveal about the cosmos. As we dive deeper into the lore of such incidents, the fabric of our collective understanding of humanity, secrecy, and exploration is ever challenged.

13.2 Community Reaction

The revelation of UFO crash sites has historically elicited a myriad of reactions from communities, often defining the local sentiment towards extraterrestrial phenomena. When the news breaks, varying degrees of skepticism, excitement, fear, and curiosity ripple through towns and cities impacted by these alleged events.

In many instances, the reactions stem from sheer disbelief at the idea of otherworldly visitation. Local residents often respond to the reports in a spectrum that ranges from indifference to fervent interest. In towns like Roswell, New Mexico—a name forever linked to UFO lore—community reaction dramatically transformed over the decades, shaping the town's identity and economic future.

Initial Responses

When a crash is reported, the first responses tend to reveal community dynamics, which can be categorized into several distinct reactions:

- **Skepticism:** The initial response often sees residents voicing doubts about the credibility of the sightings, dismissing them as hoaxes or exaggerations. Many locals rely heavily on headlines and default to scientific explanations.

- **Fear and Alarm:** Particularly in the early days of crash reports, fears of government cover-ups or potential threats from extraterrestrial beings can lead to panic within communities. Safety concerns arise, prompting questions regarding who is investigating the site and why.

- **Curiosity and Investigation:** Fascination with UFOs leads to a surge in amateur investigation. Residents often frequent crash sites as curiosity-driven tours begin to emerge, accompanied by inquiries into the existence of evidence or further sightings.

Economic Impact

The economic ramifications of perceived UFO crashes can be profound and lasting. Communities sometimes find unexpected opportunities arise from the intrigue surrounding these events. In Roswell's case:

- **Tourism Boom:** Following the alleged crash in 1947, Roswell embraced its notoriety, establishing the International UFO Museum and Research Center, which now attracts thousands of visitors annually. Shops and restaurants capitalize on this influx, creating a local economy rooted in UFO tourism.

- **Merchandising Opportunities:** Local businesses often develop a wide array of UFO-themed merchandise, engaging with the tourism boom. Items range from T-shirts to alien memorabilia, contributing to the economic landscape.

- **Media Attention:** Increased media coverage often follows a reported crash, driving interest and further bolstering local businesses eager to showcase their connection to the event.

Social Division

However, the community reaction can also polarize residents. Emotions often run high, leading to divisions within the local populace:

- **Conspiracy Theorists vs. Skeptics:** The emergence of conspiracy theorists can create friction between those who believe in the presence of extraterrestrial intelligence and those who uphold a model of scientific rationalism. Debates over what constitutes truth versus misinformation can split families, friendships, and social circles.

- **Generational Perspectives:** Younger residents may adopt more open-minded beliefs towards UFOs, while older generations may cling to traditions steeped in skepticism. This generational gap can influence community dialogues and attitudes towards such reports.

Cultural Influence

Beyond individual towns, the broader cultural impact of UFO crash narratives plays a significant role in shaping societal views:

- **Media Representation:** Documentaries, movies, and series often re-interpret the crash stories, sparking renewed interest. Such representations may glamorize these events, further blurring the lines between reality and fiction.

- **Pop Culture Integration:** References to UFO crashes infiltrate literature, music, and art, creating a dialogue that transcends local communities. Encounters morph from news stories to myth-making, deeply embedding themselves within collective consciousness.

The Ongoing Cycle

In communities that have experienced UFO reports, the cycle of reaction remains ongoing. Investigative gatherings, local newsletters, and online forums create platforms for discussion and shared experiences, maintaining the fire of curiosity and inquiry.

Regardless of whether residents believe in extraterrestrial encounters, the continual engagement around UFO crash sites reveals cultural touchstones that resonate beyond mere facts. Each sighting or crash fuels folklore and narrative, reasserting the human desire to seek understanding of the unknown.

In summary, community reactions to UFO crash sites encapsulate a complex interplay of skepticism, excitement, and social dynamics that highlight how deeply humanity grapples with the potential of life beyond Earth. As these discussions unfold, they offer invaluable insights into not just the local lore, but also our collective psyche when faced with the monumental question: Are we alone in the universe?

13.3 Government Inquiry Outcomes

The investigation into UFO crash sites has seen a plethora of governmental inquiries, each one steeped in secrecy and an air of intrigue. Over the decades, various branches of the U.S. government—as well as international authorities—have conducted investigations that not only aimed to unearth the truth behind these bizarre incidents but also to mitigate public fear and dissuade rampant conspiracy theories. This subchapter delves into the outcomes of these inquiries, revealing the stances that have been taken and the implications of their findings.

The Historical Context

The most notable government inquiry into UFO phenomena began after the Roswell incident in 1947, when reports emerged of an alleged alien spacecraft crash in New Mexico. Initially, the military claimed it had recovered a "flying disc," only to retract their statement the following day, asserting it was merely a weather balloon. This sparked a long-standing quest to investigate not only the events at Roswell but also other purported crash sites across the country.

Key Government Investigative Programs:

1. **Project Sign (1948-1949)**

Initiated to systematically evaluate the UFO phenomenon, Project Sign was responsible for analyzing reports and attempting to determine the nature of UFO sightings. The program's findings were initially classified as "unidentified," yet its overall conclusions tended to deflect the idea that UFOs posed any threat to national security.

2. **Project Grudge (1949-1951)**

A direct successor to Project Sign, Grudge actively sought to debunk UFO sightings. The aim was to reassure the public and counter rising panic. The final report of Project Grudge, however, contained many unresolved cases, hinting at the complexity of the phenomena.

3. **Project Blue Book (1952-1969)**

Lasting nearly two decades, this program compiled and analyzed thousands of UFO reports. Of the 12,618 sightings documented, 701 were left unexplained, leading to an outpouring of public curiosity and further speculation on government knowledge surrounding these events.

Outcomes and Implications

The inquiry outcomes from these governmental programs painted a complex portrait regarding UFO crashes. Several key conclusions emerged from these studies:

- **Secrecy and Public Discourse**: The continued classification of findings led to public distrust. Many individuals began to suspect that the government was concealing critical information from citizens.
- **Scientific Dismissal**: Officials from Project Blue Book often

leaned towards skepticism, arguing that most sightings were attributable to mundane phenomena—weather balloons, aircraft, or astronomical anomalies—further perpetuating the stigma surrounding credible reporting on UFOs.
- **Lack of Definitive Evidence**: Despite numerous inquiries, no definitive evidence has surfaced to confirm the existence of extraterrestrial vehicles or beings involved in crashes. The lack of verifiable proof often left more questions than answers.

Shifts in Military and Government Attitudes

In recent years, there has been a renewed interest in UFOs, catalyzed by the public release of military footage showing unidentified aerial phenomena (UAP). In 2020, the Department of Defense established a Task Force to study these sightings, leading to a report intended to summarize findings and recommend future actions. The outcomes of this task force have prompted several significant shifts:

- **Increased Transparency**: Authorities have begun to release classified documents related to UFO sightings and investigations, fostering a more open dialogue about these phenomena.
- **Legitimizing the Investigation**: By publicly acknowledging the existence of UAP, government officials have sought to modernize the conversation surrounding UFOs and renew academic research into the phenomenon.
- **Potential National Security Implications**: UAP sightings are now framed within the context of national security, elevating the importance of understanding these phenomena. The argument is that some sightings could potentially represent advanced technologies from adversary nations.

Conclusion

The outcomes of government inquiries into UFO crash sites reveal a history of evolving attitudes, scientific skepticism, and a continuously shifting narrative. While the fallout from earlier investigations often resulted in public disillusionment and concern regarding government secrecy, recent developments have opened the door to more informed discussions. As investigations move forward, the entwined narratives of government oversight, public interest, and potential extraterrestrial technology continue to captivate the curiosity of UFO enthusiasts, researchers, and conspiracy theorists alike. The quest for truth surrounding UFO crash sites remains one of the great intrigues of modern history, inviting further inquiry and speculation in the years to come.

Chapter 14: The Battle of Los Angeles

14.1 A City in Panic

As the sun set over the small town of Roswell, New Mexico, in July 1947, the quiet hum of everyday life was shattered by an event that would sow confusion, speculation, and an enduring legacy of conspiracy. News spread quickly that something extraordinary had fallen from the sky—a purported flying saucer had crashed near the desert outskirts. The following days saw a feverish rush of excitement paired with palpable fear, shaping the narrative of one of history's most famous UFO incidents.

The Initial Discovery

On July 8, 1947, the Roswell Army Air Field released a sensational press statement declaring they had recovered a "flying disc." This announcement sparked a wave of curiosity and alarm among residents. For many, the implication that extraterrestrial beings might have traversed vast distances to visit Earth was both exhilarating and disturbing. People reacted in various ways:

- **Skepticism**: Many residents dismissed the claim as a mere publicity stunt or as a misidentification of weather balloons, which were commonly used by the military for testing.
- **Fear**: Others were gripped by anxiety, fearing that this event might be part of a larger, potentially ominous presence from

outer space.

As reporters flocked to the city, the situation escalated. Journalists raced to get the scoop while local citizens shared wild stories about the crash. The incident captured the town's attention in an unprecedented manner, leading to countless speculative theories and pseudo-scientific inquiries.

Government Response

The U.S. government's response was equally chaotic. Within hours, military personnel converged on the crash site, securing the area and initiating a cleanup operation. However, as the narrative evolved, so did the official statements. Instead of corroborating the initial press release, the military abruptly changed its stance, declaring the discovery was a downed weather balloon, not a flying saucer. This retraction only fueled public intrigue and distrust.

The subtleties of government engagement added layers to the incident—there were rumors of cover-ups and silenced witnesses. An integral part of the city's panic would be the rumors surrounding military personnel, whom many believed were involved in a secretive handling of non-human materials.

Witness Accounts

As with many UFO incidents, the eyewitness accounts varied immensely, ranging from eerily consistent to fancifully exaggerated. Notably, several residents claimed to have witnessed strange lights in the sky and heard a thunderous explosion that night. Unnamed military officials purportedly described encounters at the crash site, claiming to have seen alien bodies and technology so advanced that it was beyond human comprehension. A few of the most cited reports included:

- **Frankie Rowe**, a local girl at the time, who claimed to have been taken to the crash site by her father, a firefighter. She recounted eerie details about seeing debris and suggesting

non-human entities were indeed recovered.
- **Mack Brazel**, the rancher who discovered the debris, initially reported strange wreckage to authorities and later mysteriously recanted, leading many to believe he was coerced or faced threats.

The Media Frenzy

As the story vacillated between speculation and censorship, the media's role ballooned. Newspapers, radio shows, and later television programs seized upon the story, each adding its twist to the tale. The sensationalization of UFOs became a staple of American culture, further entrenching the idea of alien visitation in the national ethos. This newfound obsession birthed an array of literature and documentaries probing into hidden truths, adding to an evolving mythology surrounding Roswell.

Lasting Legacy of Panic

The Roswell incident didn't just impact the locals; it ushered in an era of heightened interest in UFOs, leading to an explosion of UFO sightings nationwide and the burgeoning of UFO culture. Conspiracy theories proliferated, creating dedicated communities that dissected every minutia of the event. From books to conventions, the town became synonymous with the UFO phenomenon, creating a pilgrimage site for enthusiasts, researchers, and inquisitors alike.

In many ways, Roswell serves as a fascinating case study of societal panic, mass hysteria, and the pervasive nature of conspiracy. It symbolically embodies the intersection of the unknown and the known, demonstrating how fear and fascination can intertwine to transform a simple incident into a historical enigma that continues to captivate imaginations. The initial panic would eventually give way to a longstanding intrigue that few could have predicted, forever marking Roswell in the annals of UFO literature.

14.2 The Official Explanation

The fascination surrounding UFO crash sites often reveals a complex interplay between public intrigue and government response. Over the decades, many incidents have sparked speculation about extraterrestrial contact, yet official explanations have often aimed to demystify these events, guiding public perception and maintaining control over the narrative. Understanding these official stances can illuminate the cultural landscape where UFOs operate and highlight the discrepancies often present in the accounts of witnesses.

The Roswell Incident

One of the most prominent UFO crash sites in history, the Roswell incident of July 1947, serves as a pivotal study in official explanations. Initially reported as a "flying disc" recovery by the Roswell Army Air Field, the U.S. military quickly retracted this statement. Instead, they asserted that the recovered debris was from a downed weather balloon, specifically part of Project Mogul—an initiative aimed at detecting Soviet nuclear tests. This shift in explanation left many questioning the authenticity of the information provided by the military.

Important points regarding the official stance on Roswell include:

- **Rapid Response**: The military's swift alteration of its narrative from a "flying disc" to a mundane weather balloon fueled conspiracy theories.
- **Disappearing Evidence**: Key eyewitness accounts were either discredited or mysteriously vanished, leading to suspicion about the authenticity of the government's claims.
- **Cultural Impact**: The conflicting narratives about Roswell have nurtured a continuous stream of interest in UFOs, showcasing a public hunger for answers.

The Air Force's Reports

In 1969, the United States Air Force concluded its investigations into UFOs through Project Blue Book, which focused primarily on sightings categorized as "unidentified" or "explainable." The final report argued that the majority of UFO reports could be attributed to:

- **Natural Phenomena**: Lights and objects often identified as UFOs were frequently later understood to be atmospheric conditions, such as lenticular clouds or meteorological events.
- **Misidentifications**: Reports of unidentified aerial phenomena could often be traced back to human error or a lack of knowledge regarding conventional aircraft and other technologies.
- **Military Aircraft**: Many UFO sightings were deemed to be actual military craft, particularly given the classified nature of many Air Force operations at the time.

The Air Force emphasized that no evidence of extraterrestrial life existed. However, the report's conclusions have done little to extinguish conspiracy theories and public fascination.

Modern Investigative Entities

Despite these official explanations, newer entities like the Pentagon's Unidentified Aerial Phenomena (UAP) Task Force have emerged, which challenge long-standing narratives. Established to further investigate military sightings of unidentified objects, the task force seemingly contradicts previous governmental claims that dismissed the significance of UFO sightings. Key takeaways from their stance are:

- **Acknowledgment of Sightings**: The UAP Task Force recognized that many encounters reported by military personnel remain unexplained to this day.
- **Call for Transparency**: This new era within U.S. defense

institutions has pushed for greater transparency regarding military encounters with aerial phenomena, contradicting the more secretive approaches of the past.
- **Public Engagement**: The modern push for disclosure and public engagement suggests a shift from ridicule towards genuinely considering the implications of unexplained aerial phenomena.

The Influence of Popular Culture

The discrepancies between official explanations and public interest highlight an enduring gap. Documentaries, books, and movies continue to explore themes around UFO crashed sites, often portraying government agencies as antagonists withholding the truth. This cultural portrayal influences perceptions, leading many to question the integrity of the information provided.

Conclusion

The official explanations regarding UFO crash sites reveal a tapestry of governmental communication strategies, media interactions, and cultural phenomena. These narratives serve dual purposes: to assuage public fear and curiosity while simultaneously protecting sensitive information. As investigations evolve, the dialogue between authorities and UFO enthusiasts grows increasingly complex, pointing towards a future where the line between official declarations and public speculation may blur even further. Serious researchers and enthusiasts alike are urged to continue examining these narratives critically to uncover the broader implications surrounding UFO phenomena.

14.3 Lasting Mysteries and Theories

Throughout history, various reports of UFO crash sites have given way to an array of lasting mysteries and theories that continue to provoke both fascination and speculation. From Roswell to more modern encounters, these sites are often wrapped in layers of intrigue, conspiracy, and unanswered questions that fuel ongoing investigations and debates among enthusiasts, historians, and conspiracy theorists alike.

One of the most notable crash sites in UFO lore is the infamous Roswell incident of 1947. Initially reported as a "flying disc" recovery, the U.S. military quickly retracted that statement, claiming instead that it was a downed weather balloon. This sudden change sparked public suspicion and laid the groundwork for countless theories. To this day, enthusiasts examine the details of Roswell and other crash sites to deduce what really happened.

Key Theories Surrounding UFO Crash Sites

The mysteries surrounding UFO crash sites often lead to varied theories that range from plausible to far-fetched. Here are some of the most enduring theories:

- **Government Cover-Up**: Many believe that governments, especially the United States, have retrieved alien technology from crashed UFOs and are concealing this information to maintain control over advanced technology. This theory gained traction with reports like the alleged recovery of an extraterrestrial craft at Roswell and claims made by former military personnel.

- **Reverse Engineering of Alien Technology**: Some theorists argue that, rather than merely covering up the existence of UFOs, governments are actively reverse-engineering alien technology for military or civilian applications. Such claims suggest that advancements in areas such as radar, stealth technology, and even computer design may stem from recovered alien artifacts.

- **Life Forms on Board**: Another widely circulated theory

revolves around the possibility of extraterrestrial life being involved in these crash incidents. This notion often captures public attention, with theories suggesting that beings aboard these crafts may have been recovered for study, either alive or dead.

- **Interdimensional Travel**: Some researchers propose that UFOs do not only hail from other planets but also from different dimensions or timelines. This theory postulates that UFO crashes could be the result of failed interdimensional travel, leading to accidental appearances in our reality.

- **Hoaxes and Misidentifications**: Not all theories surrounding UFO crash sites hinge on extraterrestrial involvement. Some suggest that many reports are based on misidentifications of natural phenomena, military tests, or outright hoaxes. This perspective urges a more skeptical examination of eyewitness accounts and physical evidence.

Notable UFO Crash Sites and Their Mysteries

1. **Roswell, New Mexico (1947)**: The key event that ignited UFO fever, when a supposed flying disc crashed, but was immediately reclassified by the military as a weather balloon.

2. **Kecksburg, Pennsylvania (1965)**: Witnesses reported a bell-shaped object crashing in the woods. The military's rapid response and subsequent cleanup fostered theories of a cover-up.

3. **The Rendlesham Forest Incident (1980)**: Multiple U.S. Air Force personnel claimed to have witnessed unusual lights in the forest near military bases in England. Some even reported seeing a craft land, but officials have denied the existence of any concrete evidence.

4. **The 1980 Brazilian Incident (Varginha)**: This case involves claims of a UFO crash and the alleged capture of extraterrestrial beings by Brazilian authorities, which still lack official acknowledgment or resolution.

The Impact of Lasting Mysteries

The profound mysteries surrounding UFO crash sites do more than just spark theories; they also play a vital role in reshaping public perception of government transparency, scientific inquiry, and humanity's place in the universe. As rumors swirl and information is either released or withheld, the intrigue surrounding UFO phenomena grows. Theories continue to evolve as new evidence, be it physical artifacts or credible testimonies, comes to light.

Moreover, these mysteries have engendered a thriving community of researchers and enthusiasts who examine every detail with a fine-tooth comb. This investigative spirit is fueled by various motivations—whether they are seeking the truth, craving excitement, or searching for validation of their beliefs regarding life beyond Earth.

While definitive resolutions remain elusive, the study of UFO crash sites serves as a mirror reflecting our age-old quest to uncover the unknown. This pursuit of knowledge—often obscured by conspiracy and secrecy—ensures that the mysteries encompassing these sites will continue to engage and challenge future generations.

Chapter 15: Recent Developments in UFO Crashes

15.1 The 21st Century Paradigm Shift

In the early decades of the 21st century, the world witnessed an expansion in the discourse surrounding UFOs, particularly in the context of UFO crash sites. This paradigm shift can be attributed to several converging factors, including technological advancements, cultural changes, and renewed governmental transparency. These elements have not only reshaped the conversation about UFOs but have also sparked greater interest in specific incidents historically associated with crashes purportedly involving extraterrestrial vehicles.

Advances in Technology and Information Access

One of the most significant contributors to this shift has been the advent of the internet and digital technology. Researchers, enthusiasts, and everyday citizens gained unprecedented access to information, allowing for:

- **Global Collaboration**: Online forums and social media platforms enabled UFO enthusiasts to collaborate across countries and share findings instantaneously.
- **Digital Archives**: Many governments and organizations have digitized archives, making documents related to UFO

sightings and crash sites more accessible than ever before. This democratization of information has empowered amateur investigators.

- **Research Tools**: Technology such as Geographic Information Systems (GIS) and drones have transformed the way investigations are conducted. ArcGIS programs and aerial reconnaissance help enthusiasts map UFO sightings and crash locations in ways that were unimaginable just a decade ago.

Cultural Shifts Toward Openness

As decades passed, societal skepticism towards UFO phenomena has seen a notable decline. Increased openness in popular culture, reflected in films, television shows, and internet media, has generated enthusiasm for the topic. This cultural embrace can be summarized by a few key trends:

- **Mainstream Media Take**: Outlets like The New York Times and major news channels began reporting serious investigations, prompting a more balanced understanding of sightings and historical crash sites.
- **Documentary Influence**: Documentaries exploring renowned crash incidents, such as Roswell and Kecksburg, have reignited public interest and spurred legitimate inquiries regarding what lies behind governmental secrecy.
- **Public Figures and Disclosure**: Various public figures, including former military personnel and politicians, have come forward with claims related to UFOs and crash sites, increasing the credibility of the subject in the eyes of the public.

Government Accountability and Disclosure Initiatives

Governmental secrecy regarding UFO crash sites has long been a source of skepticism among UFO enthusiasts and conspiracy theorists alike. However, the 21st century has marked a momentous shift in how governments in various countries, particularly the United States, have begun to address the phenomena. Key occurrences of governmental shift include:

- **U.A.P. Task Force**: The establishment of the Unidentified Aerial Phenomena (UAP) Task Force by the Pentagon in 2020 indicated a serious commitment to disclose information about encounters with unidentified flying objects, including crashes.
- **Congressional Hearings**: In 2021, congressional hearings on UAPs drew significant media attention, illuminating the reality that the government had been studying phenomena that cannot be easily explained.
- **Declassified Documents**: The release of declassified documents by the Pentagon regarding past UFO incidents has reinvigorated investigations into locations of alleged crashes, now supported by former military witnesses and corroborated evidence.

New Investigative Approaches

The changing dynamics of how UFO phenomena are approached in both public discourse and investigative endeavors have inspired fresh approaches to the study of UFO crash sites. Some of these methods include:

- **Forensic Investigations**: Historians and paranormal

investigators increasingly apply forensic methodologies to UFO crash sites, analyzing soil samples and conducting ground-penetrating radar surveys to search for physical evidence.
- **Crowdsourced Investigations**: Citizen scientists utilizing online platforms to reconstruct and analyze reported sightings, including potential crash sites, are creating a more comprehensive mapping of alleged incidents around the world.
- **Interdisciplinary Studies**: The incorporation of various academic disciplines, including psychology, sociology, and engineering, enriches discussions and analyses surrounding UFO phenomena, potentially providing new insights into the cultural implications of these events.

Conclusion

The 21st-century paradigm shift marks a significant turning point in the investigation of UFO crash sites. As technology improves, cultural narratives evolve, and government transparency increases, the landscape of UFO research continues to broaden. The interplay of these factors is giving rise to a new era in which the search for understanding our unidentified flying companions is more vigorous, more collaborative, and ultimately more credible than ever before. This evolution leaves us on the cusp of potential discoveries that could change how we perceive not just UFOs, but the very fabric of our reality.

15.2 New Government Acknowledgments

In recent years, the acknowledgment of unidentified flying objects (UFOs) by various government entities has taken a significant leap from speculation and secrecy to transparency and admission. This newfound openness has been fueled by mounting public interest, advancements in technology, and the implications of biological, extraterrestrial encounters, urging officials to confront these phenomena head-on. Here, we explore the specific government acknowledgments related to UFO crash sites and their wider implications for our understanding of aerial phenomena.

Historically, the relationship between UFO incidents and government responses has oscillated between denial and intrigue. However, during the past couple of decades, a palpable shift has been observed. Several high-profile reports and public testimonies have cut through the fog of skepticism, ushering in a new era of investigation. This transition indicates an acknowledgment that profound and mysterious events like UFO crashes deserve serious examination and validation.

Key Moments of Government Acknowledgment

1. **The 2017 New York Times Revelation**: With the unveiling of the Pentagon's Advanced Aerospace Threat Identification Program (AATIP), the public gained access to compelling evidence regarding military encounters with UFOs. Video footage released by the U.S. Navy showing unidentified flying objects behaving in ways that defied conventional physics prompted a discussion not merely about aerial sightings but also potential crash sites and the retrieval of alien technology.

2. **UFO Report of June 2021**: Following the Pentagon's directive to release information regarding UFO sightings, the Office of the Director of National Intelligence (ODNI) presented a report that discussed 144 incidents of unexplained aerial phenomena. While the report stopped short of confirming extraterrestrial origins, it acknowledged certain events where objects exhibited behavior suggestive of advanced technology, indirectly pointing to the possibility of past crash sites needing investigation.

3. **Whistleblower Testimonies**: Throughout the years, various individuals—ranging from former military personnel to government officials—have come forward with accounts of encounters with UFOs and alleged crash sites. Notable figures such as Luis Elizondo, a former AATIP director, openly discuss the importance of examining potential wreckage linked to these phenomena.

Implications of These Acknowledgments

The acknowledgment of UFOs and related crash sites by government entities raises several profound implications:

- **Increased Research Funding**: The legitimacy granted to UFO phenomena has led to a potential realignment of research resources, allowing scientists and investigators to study crash sites more systematically and methodically.

- **Shift in Public Perception**: As governments recognize the importance of investigating unexplained aerial phenomena, public skepticism is gradually decreasing. Acceptance of the unknown opens dialogues around intelligence and communication with entities beyond our planet.

- **Interdisciplinary Collaboration**: The complexities surrounding UFO crash sites call for collaboration across various fields, including astrophysics, engineering, archaeology, and anthropology. A multifaceted approach ensures a comprehensive understanding of any recovered materials and their context.

Legislative Action and Future Investigations

In light of these government acknowledgments, new legislative measures are emerging aimed at transparency surrounding UFO data:

- **Establishment of the Unidentified Aerial Phenomena (UAP) Task Force**: In 2020, the U.S. Department of Defense established a task force dedicated to assessing reports of UFOs. This entity is tasked with investigating the source and nature of these phenomena as well as establishing procedures for analyzing potential crash sites.

- **Continued Public Pressure**: The increase in UFO enthusiasts, historians, conspiracy theorists, and researchers has resulted in heightened public interest and pressure on governments to disclose historical documents related to alleged crash sites. This public push promotes a culture of accountability and encourages broader framing of UFOs as pertinent to national security and human understanding.

Conclusion

The dialogue surrounding UFO crash sites has evolved dramatically thanks to recent government acknowledgments, prompting a deeper investigation into the mysteries of our skies. While substantial evidence remains to be discovered, the ongoing commitment from officials to clarify UFO phenomena fosters hope that we may soon unravel the enigma of aerial mysteries that have long captivated not only our imaginations but also our history. As both government bodies and citizens advocate for transparency, the opportunities for groundbreaking research into UFO crash sites have never been more promising. To understand what lies ahead, one must not only look up at the stars, but also delve into the archives of history that may reveal more than what is merely seen.

15.3 The Future of UFO Investigations

The landscape of UFO investigations has dramatically evolved over the decades, shifting from a fringe hobbyist interest to a more structured and scientifically inclined field. As the stigma surrounding discussions of unidentified flying objects begins to dissipate, the future of UFO investigations—particularly regarding crash sites—holds both promise and uncertainty.

Advancements in Technology

The technological progression plays a pivotal role in how we approach the mysteries of UFO crash sites. Modern tools and methodologies offer researchers an unprecedented ability to analyze evidence and document findings. Consider the following advancements:

- **Drones and Aerial Imaging**: Drones equipped with advanced imaging technology can survey suspected crash sites from various angles, capturing high-resolution photographs and thermal imagery to identify unusual temperature anomalies—often indicating recent or ongoing disturbances in the environment.

- **Geospatial Analysis**: GIS (Geographic Information Systems) allows researchers to visualize, interpret, and analyze spatial data related to crash sites. By layering multiple data sources—like satellite imagery, topographical maps, and eyewitness reports—investigators can develop a clearer understanding of geographical correlations and incident patterns.

- **Laboratory Technology**: The use of advanced materials science has transformed how we study samples that might be linked to UFOs. Techniques like mass spectrometry and electron microscopy allow for detailed analysis of purported materials from alleged crash sites, providing insight into their composition and origin.

Collaborative Research

The future of UFO investigations may increasingly rely on collaboration among various fields of study:

- **Interdisciplinary Approach**: Researchers from diverse disciplines, including physics, engineering, anthropology, and environmental science, can contribute unique perspectives to the investigation of crash sites. This holistic approach allows for a deeper understanding of the incidents and helps bridge gaps in knowledge.

- **Government and Private Sector Partnerships**: As more governments around the world acknowledge the need for transparency regarding UFO phenomena, partnerships may form between public agencies and private research organizations. Such collaborations could lead to streamlined investigations, shared resources, and databases containing previously classified or obscure information.

Public Interest and Crowdsourcing

The role of the public in UFO investigations is set to expand. With the growth of digital media and social networks, individuals can participate in monitoring and investigations as never before:

- **Crowdsourced Investigation**: Online platforms can host collaborative projects where enthusiasts analyze video footage, share testimonies, and contribute to documenting sightings or crash reports. This communal effort may uncover new leads or reveal patterns that individual researchers might overlook.

- **Citizen Science Projects**: Similar to projects where the public helps analyze astronomical data, citizen science initiatives could arise to engage non-professionals in studying crash sites. This democratization of research may lead to breakthroughs driven by collective input from various backgrounds and skill sets.

Ethical Considerations

The potential for discoveries related to UFOs, including their crash sites, raises important ethical questions that researchers will need to navigate. Future investigations must prioritize:

- **Respect for Cultural Sites**: Many alleged crash sites are located near indigenous or culturally significant areas. Investigators must conduct their work with sensitivity and respect for the traditions of local communities and ensure that their activities do not cause harm.

- **Transparency and Integrity**: As more data becomes available, researchers have an obligation to uphold standards of transparency and integrity in their findings. This includes the responsible reporting of evidence, the recognition of established scientific principles, and the acknowledgment of biases that could color interpretations.

The Quest for Evidence

Lastly, the pursuit of tangible evidence continues to be a driving force in the field of UFO investigations. As skepticism persists, a systematic approach to evidence collection and analysis will be essential:

- **Standardized Protocols**: Establishing protocols that outline how crash sites should be examined and evidence cataloged will help to legitimize findings. Increased consistency can lead to more reliable data, paving the way for future analyses and discussions.

- **Peer Review**: Like in any scientific field, a robust peer review process is vital. As researchers present their findings on crash sites, they must be subject to scrutiny by their peers to ensure that the claims made are substantiated and that methodologies are sound.

The future of UFO investigations, particularly those linked to crash sites, will undoubtedly be marked by scientific rigor, technological advancements, collaboration, and ethical responsibility. As we stand on the threshold of what could be groundbreaking discoveries, the convergence of curiosity and investigation inspires hope for a greater understanding of our universe's mysteries.

Thank you for journeying through the fascinating world of UFO crash sites with us. Your interest fuels ongoing research and discovery. For further insights, please visit my Amazon Author page: https://www.amazon.com/author/jadesummers and explore my personal website at https://www.triptroveguides.com/.

About the Author

Welcome to My Official Author Page!
About Me

Hello! I'm Jade Summers, a 21-year-old author from the USA with a passion for blending technology and travel into my writing. I use ChatGPT daily, which has inspired me to create insightful and accessible e-books for professionals across diverse industries. My love for travel also drives me to explore and share the wonders of various destinations around the world.

Growing up in the digital age, I've seamlessly integrated technology into my life and travels, making me uniquely qualified to guide others on using AI in their professional lives and to help travelers discover new experiences around the globe.

My Work

I'm thrilled to announce my ambitious plans to publish two long series of e-books. One series focuses on the application of ChatGPT across different professional sectors, helping professionals harness AI's power. The other series is dedicated to travel, featuring guides on popular places, attractions, and activities in various countries and towns worldwide.

Here are some examples of what you can look forward to:
Professional Series: Titles like "ChatGPT for Education," "ChatGPT for Healthcare Providers," and "ChatGPT for Marketers," among 300+ other books. **Travel Series:** Titles like "Hot Springs in Iceland," "Food Tasting Tours in Mexico," and "River Cruises in the Amazon," also among 300+ planned guides.

What to Expect Next

Stay tuned for the release of my titles and join me in exploring the extensive potential of ChatGPT in the professional world and the enchanting beauty of global travel. Each book promises to open new horizons, whether you're adapting to AI in your career or seeking your next vacation destination.

As an author, I'm here to bridge the gap between technology and real-world experiences, guiding professionals and travelers alike through the evolving landscapes of their careers and journeys. Whether you're diving into the world of AI or exploring the rich cultures of our world, my books are designed to be your gateway to new possibilities. Join me, and let's explore the potential of ChatGPT and the beauty of our planet, one book at a time.

Read more at https://www.triptroveguides.com/.

Printed in Great Britain
by Amazon